THE SWORD OF NO-SWORD

Yamaoka Tesshu, age fifty-two.

The Sword of No-Sword

LIFE OF THE MASTER WARRIOR TESSHU

John Stevens

SHAMBHALA
BOSTON & LONDON 1994

Shambhala Publications, Inc.
Horticultural Hall
300 Massachusetts Avenue
Boston, Massachusetts 02115

9 8 7 6 5 4 3 2 1
Printed in the United States of America on acid-free paper ⊗
Distributed in the United States by Random House, Inc., and in Canada by Random House of Canada Ltd

Library of Congress Cataloging-in-Publication Data
Stevens, John, 1947–
    The sword of no sword.
    1. Yamaoka, Tesshū, 1836–1888.   2. Swordsmen—Japan—
Biography.   3. Japan—Officials and employees—Biography.
I. Title
DS881.5 Y332S73   1984   952.03'1'0924[B]   84-5468
ISBN 1-57062-050-4

Text design/Bea Ferrigno-Lee
Cover/Eje Wray

CREDITS
Photographs not mentioned here are from private collections whose owners
    prefer to remain anonymous.
Shumpukan Bunko, pages 101, 104–105.
Zensho-an Treasury, pages 3, 19, 55, 58, 80, 83, 89, 94–96, 102, 104, 161.
Zuiganji Treasury, pages 69, 71, 94.
Tesshuji Treasury, pages 67, 77.
Eisei Bunko, page 61, middle.
Yokoji Buddha Hall, page 62.
Yokoji Treasury, page 163, top.
Matsushima Kanrantei Museum, page 163, bottom.
Engakuji Treasury, page 164.
Takahashi Family, page 106.

CONTENTS

FOREWORD

Yamaoka Tesshu was an outstanding figure of the turbulent era that marked the birth of modern Japan. In the public sphere, Tesshu negotiated with Saigo Takamori and arranged for the peaceful transfer of power from the old order to the new; as an individual student of the Ways, Tesshu attained profound enlightenment at the age of forty-five and realized the inner principles of swordsmanship, Zen, and calligraphy. Thereafter, Tesshu was like Miyamoto Musashi, "passing one's days without attachment to any particular Way" (*Book of Five Rings*). Tesshu too became an extraordinarily versatile and prolific master: a peerless swordsman who established the No-Sword School; a wise and compassionate Zen teacher in the Tekisui tradition; and an unrivaled calligrapher who gathered all things of heaven and earth in his brush. Even today, nearly a century after his death, Tesshu's incredible vitality can still be discerned in his brushwork. If viewed properly, the tremendous transformation accompanying Tesshu's awakening and the progressive deepening of his enlightened insight during the last eight years of his life are clearly evident in his calligraphy.

Musashi, samurai artist supreme, is perhaps the only other practitioner who similarly penetrated the essence of so many different Ways; unlike Musashi, whose real story is difficult to ascertain, much more reliable information is available on Tesshu, so it is thus possible to form an accurate picture of the man and his teaching.

Since there is no better exemplar of the spirit of Zen than Yamaoka Tesshu, I am pleased that John Stevens Sensei has prepared this definitive English language biography of that great master. While working together on the translation of my book *Zen and the Art of Calligraphy* and several other projects, I have developed a high regard for Stevens Sensei's wide-ranging knowledge and perceptive understanding of Oriental culture. A fine scholar and accomplished martial art practitioner, he well embodies the samurai ideal of *Bunbu Ryodo*, a student of the classics as well as the martial arts. Furthermore, Stevens Sensei's dedication to Tesshu's spirit is total.

The true value of any enlightened master's teaching transcends national barriers; with the publication of this study, Tesshu's message will now be a guide for dedicated practitioners in all lands.

Terayama Tanchu (Katsujo)
Headmaster, Hitsuzen Society
Lecturer, Sophia University
Author of *Tesshu and Calligraphy*
(*Tesshu to Shodo*); *Hitsuzendo*;
and *Zen and the Art of Calligraphy*

PREFACE

Like most of those attracted to the life and teaching of Yamaoka Tesshu, I was initially interested in him as a martial artist. Tesshu was swordsman nonpareil to be sure, and anyone who truly wishes to understand *budo*, the Way of Martial Valor, must be thoroughly acquainted with the principles of his No-Sword School. However, during the course of my many years of research on Tesshu, I gradually realized that he was far more than a talented swordsman—in addition to being among the finest calligraphers of any age, Tesshu is one of the greatest of all enlightened Buddhist laymen.

Perhaps the only comparable figure in Japan is the sixteenth century swordsman Miyamoto Musashi, well-known to American readers of *The Book of Five Rings* and the novel *Musashi*. Unlike Musashi, whose fame rests mainly on legend and highly fictionalized accounts of his life, Tesshu is much closer to us in time and temperament, well-acquainted with Western thought, European science, and the realities of world politics. Furthermore, even though the era in which Tesshu lived was nearly as violent as that of Musashi, Tesshu never resorted to the ruthless cut-the-enemy-down-by-any-means tactics of Musashi, disarming his opponents instead with the power of "no-sword."

In the twentieth century, practice of Tesshu's three *do*—the Way of the Sword, the Way of Zen, and the Way of the Brush—transcends national barriers. Training halls in these disciplines are found all over the world, and it is my firm belief that none of these three Ways can properly develop without correct appreciation of Tesshu's multifarious teachings.

The influence of those teachings continues. A recent prime minister of Japan, Nakasone Yasuhiro, is said to be an ardent fan of Tesshu. Whenever this prime minister had a break in his busy schedule, he did zazen—accompanied by bodyguards alertly perched on the meditation cushions beside him—at Zensho-an, a temple founded by Tesshu in Tokyo.

This book is a sister publication of *Abundant Peace: The Biography of Morihei Ueshiba, Founder of Aikido.* Tesshu and Morihei are the two pillars of modern budo: men of culture and religious inspiration who attained invincibility through hard training and ceaseless introspection. Neither drew a drop of blood and both stressed harmony and love over conflict and vindictiveness. Their message to us is one of peace, peace acquired in the midst of raging storms.

John Stevens
Sendai, Japan
September, 1988

AUTHOR'S NOTE

There are a number of biographies of Tesshu in Japanese, but even the most reliable are marred by inconsistencies, contradictions, and historical impossibilities. The main difficulty is that the sources are, at best, third-hand accounts, i.e., compilations by Tesshu's disciples' disciples. Tesshu rebuffed requests for an autobiography; high-minded and devoid of petty concern for his standing, Tesshu was not interested in writing a self-adulatory rendition of his life—"What is significant will endure; what is not will perish."

Working closely with the three top experts on Tesshu today—Omori Sogen, Murakami Yasumasa, and Terayama Katsujo—I have carefully sifted through all the material, separating fact from fiction, to produce this comprehensive study. I do not maintain, of course, that every story recounted here occurred exactly as described. Many, in fact, are composites of differing versions. Nevertheless, I am confident that each account accurately reflects the event in question and that it faithfully represents Tesshu's teaching.

Names are given in the Japanese manner, that is, family name first. Japanese words are italicized the first time they appear in the text and are thereafter printed in regular type.

I am extremely grateful to Prof. Terayama Katsujo and Dr. Murakami Yasumasa for providing me with so much: kind instruction, constant encouragement, invaluable advice, and priceless illustrations. Special thanks go to Hirai Genkyo of Zensho-an, Horiuchi Soshun of Zuiganji, and Yashiki Chijo of Yokoji who assisted me with obtaining photographs of pieces in the treasure houses of their respective temples. I was also fortunate to have received the gracious cooperation of the late Chief Justice Ishida Kazuto. Emily Hilburn of Shambhala was a considerate and thorough editor and president Samuel Bercholz has my gratitude for supporting the publication of this ten-year project.

1

TESSHU'S LIFE AND TIMES

After two hundred and fifty years of relative calm and isolation, the once mighty Tokugawa Shogunate was tottering. Established in 1603 by Ieyasu, the last of the "Three Unifiers"—the other two being Oda Nobunaga and Toyotomi Hideyoshi—the regime followed a rigid closed-door policy. By 1640, all foreign missionaries were expelled from the country (native Christians who did not recant were executed) and, with the exception of a tiny Dutch concession, all overseas trade was suspended.

The island nation flourished in the peace and security of the early years of the Tokugawa reign, but by 1830 a number of factors had undermined the economy: strict adherence to a four-tier social system (samurai-peasant-craftsman-merchant); a cumbersome and inefficient bureaucracy; huge deficits incurred by both the national and local governments, caused in part by the ruinously expensive requirement that all *daimyo* (feudal lords) maintain households in the capital city of Edo; repeated crop failures, widespread famine, and food riots.

On top of all this, Russia, England, and the United States were ominously probing Japan's coastal waters with their powerful men-of-war, demanding that the Shogunate open up the country to foreign intercourse.

Against this background of uncertainty and crisis, Ono Tetsutaro—later known as Yamaoka Tesshu—was born in Edo on June 10, 1836. His father, Ono Asaemon, was a fairly high-ranking Tokugawa retainer with a good income of 600 *koku*. (One koku was approximately five bushels of rice; it represented the standard medium of exchange and measure of wealth in the Tokugawa period.) Tesshu took after his mother Iso, a tall, solidly built woman of dark beauty. Spirited yet tender, she was the daughter of a Shinto priest at the famous Kashima Shrine. Although the sixty-three-year-old Asaemon had a number of children, natural and adopted, from previous unions, he considered the twenty-six-year-old Iso to be his "official" wife and her children to be his legal heirs. Thus, even though Tesshu was Asaemon's fourth boy, he was designated head son. (Asaemon fathered five more boys over the next fourteen years until his death at age seventy-nine.)

Tesshu passed the first ten years of his life in Edo. In 1845, his father was assigned to a new post in the Hida district and the family moved to the lovely mountain town of Takayama. There Tesshu began earnest study of the samurai curriculum: classical learning and martial arts. In addition, his father urged him to practice Zen in order to develop *fudo-shin*, the "imperturbable mind" a true samurai needed.

Tesshu always aimed high, even as a child. Once a neighbor invited the Ono family over to feast on eels, a special delicacy. Tesshu declined and remained at home. When asked why he preferred his books to a succulent meal of roasted eels, the boy replied, "Why should I waste time dining on worms? If they served up a whale then I would go!"

Although a keen student of Confucianism, Tesshu was more attracted to Buddhism; from an early age, he was a devotee of both zazen and Kannon, the Goddess of Compassion. Morning and evening, Tesshu never failed to offer tea and cakes to his small Kannon image. When he was fifteen, Tesshu, acting as his aged father's representative, made an obligatory pilgrimage to Ise Shrine. It was a long arduous journey, carried out on foot and, that particular year, in a constant downpour. Near the end of the trip, following an especially exhausting day, Tesshu failed to appear for dinner at the inn. He was discovered, still soaking wet, face down before his little Kannon statue. When Tesshu had touched the floor to make a prostration he had fallen fast asleep.

Portrait of white-robed Kannon with the Heart Sutra brushed in cursive script. Kannon, symbol of unlimited compassion, freely manifests herself in countless forms to save sentient beings. Like the willow branch in the vase next to her, Kannon is supple yet strong, fresh yet stable.

In other ways, this pilgrimage was more eye-opening. It was Tesshu's first opportunity to meet samurai and scholars from other parts of the country and to learn about the real situation of the nation.

In 1851, Tesshu's mother died of a stroke at age forty-one, leaving six sons, one a nursing infant. Since Tesshu's father, then an ailing seventy-eight-year-old, was incapable of handling family affairs, Tesshu took charge. He arranged for a wet nurse for the baby during the day and cared for his father and brothers. After everyone was in bed for the night, Tesshu would visit his mother's grave, offering fresh cakes, chanting sutras, and "talking" with her till daybreak. (This went on for fifty days, a traditional period of mourning.) Half a year later, Asaemon died, making Tesshu and his brothers orphans. Fortunately, Asaemon left a sizable estate of 3,500 *ryo*. (One ryo was a gold coin roughly equal in value to one koku.) Tesshu was able to place his brothers with various relatives and divided the inheritance among them, keeping only 100 ryo for his own use.

These affairs settled, seventeen-year-old Tesshu decided to return to Edo. After arriving in Edo in 1853, Tesshu continued his intense study of swordsmanship. He also began familiarizing himself with some of the other eighteen classical martial arts. Tesshu enrolled in both the government-sponsored Kobukan Military Institute and the Yamaoka School of spear fighting (*sojutsu*).

Yamaoka Seizan was one of the finest masters of the era. As a youth he followed the standard samurai curriculum of budo and classical learning but at nineteen abandoned all other pursuits to concentrate on the spear. In his early twenties Seizan was enlightened to the inner principles of the art after meeting wave after wave of attackers for twenty-four straight hours. His zeal for hard training was legendary. Summer or winter he wore only the same thin cotton uniform and subsisted on the simplest food. He executed as many as 30,000 thrusts in a single day and frequently trained all night with a twenty-pound spear. Once, after a four-hour match with another master, Seizan discovered his spear tip worn down four inches from his tremendous thrusts.

Seizan was much more than a fierce warrior. He was a model of filial piety, devoted to the care of his widowed mother, gently massaging her shoulders and sitting up with her in the evening to gaze at the moon. Seizan's motto was "Do not speak of others' faults; do not boast about yourself; never expect anything for services rendered; never forget kindnesses received." He once told his disciples: "If you want to attain true victory, broaden your understanding of virtue. No enemy can defeat a man of superior virtue. Attempting to win through exclusive reliance on technique will lead you nowhere."

Regrettably, soon after Tesshu's enrollment in the dojo, Seizan died of heart failure while defending a friend under attack. The nobility of Seizan's character, however, made a lasting impression on Tesshu.

Following Seizan's death, there were strange reports of an apparition lurking in the cemetery. Seizan's brother, Deishu, went to investigate. While he sat quietly out of sight in the darkness, a fierce storm blew up. As the rain poured down and the lightning flashed, a huge figure suddenly approached Seizan's grave, bowed deeply, removed his coat, and placed it around Seizan's tombstone. "Don't worry, Sensei," Deishu heard a familiar voice say in reassuring tones, "Tetsutaro is here now and everything will be all right." (Seizan, fearless in combat, was terrified of thunder.) Tesshu's devotion to his parents and teachers knew nothing of the barriers erected by death.

Seizan died a bachelor, leaving no heir. He had two brothers, but one was deaf and the other (Deishu) had previously been adopted into the maternal Takahashi clan because that family lacked a male heir. Fusako, Seizan's sixteen-year-old sister, would have to marry soon in order to have her husband assume the Yamaoka name. She reportedly told her brother Deishu: "If I cannot marry Ono Tetsutaro I will die." Nonplussed—what did his sister see in that penniless trainee whose nickname was "Ragged Tetsu?"—Deishu consulted with the family elders. Since Fusako would not relent and Tesshu agreed to the match, the two were married in 1855.

(Shinkichi, the deaf brother, carried on the family tradition as a spear-fighter. Years later, Tesshu arranged for Shinkichi to give a demonstration before the emperor. After thrusting his opponent, a senior instructor of another school, to the floor, Shinkichi kept up the attack because he was unable to hear the opponent's cry of submission. Tesshu had to grab Shinkichi's wooden spear to stop the contest.)

Following his marriage, Tesshu became more involved with politics. The kendo training halls in Edo were gathering places for *shishi* ("men of determination"), young displaced samurai who rallied around the slogan *sonno-joi*, "Revere the emperor, expel the barbarians."

In 1853, the year after Tesshu had returned to Edo, an American fleet of menacing "black ships" commanded by Matthew Perry anchored off Uraga and demanded the right to deliver a letter from President Fillmore to the leader of Japan. In better times, the Tokugawa Shogun might have been able to live up to his title of "Barbarian-subduing Generalissimo," but by now his rule was so weakened by internal dissension that he was powerless to refuse Perry's demand. An initial treaty with the Americans was negotiated in 1854. Four years later, a treaty granting full diplomatic relations, open trade, and other important concessions was signed.

In reaction to the forced opening of the country, Tesshu and a group of other *ronin* (masterless samurai) formed the Sonno-joi Party. "Revere the emperor" was originally a call to revive the flagging spirit of self-sacrifice and loyalty to the traditional leader of the nation; "expel the barbarians" was more a battle cry designed to stiffen the country's resolve against colonization by Western powers than a rational policy—given the circumstances there was no possibility of driving out foreigners. During the years 1853–1868, confusion reigned supreme: the Shogunate disintegrated; allegiances shifted daily; the economy crumbled under the pressures of foreign trade; acts of terrorism and assassination were rife; finally, there was civil war.

Steamship with the inscription, "Riding the great winds, shattering the waves of ten thousand leagues." The clock cannot be turned back and one should not be afraid of change. Developments in technology, too, must be used to expand one's horizons.

Since the old order was unable to deal with the deteriorating situation, it was energetic young samurai such as Tesshu who took control. An accomplished swordsman who stood over six feet tall and weighed some two hundred forty pounds, Tesshu was a natural leader. He joined the Shogunate as a minor official in 1856, authored a variety of pamphlets on political affairs, and by 1863 he was a recognized ronin spokesman.

It was a wild time with hundreds of ambitious samurai vying with each other on all levels, from the sublime to the ridiculous. Regardless of what it was, Tesshu did not like to be second to anyone.

Once during a drinking bout, a senior member of Tesshu's group announced, "This morning I'm going to make a one-day round trip to Narita on foot. Anyone care to join me?" Tesshu alone volunteered to join the braggart on the ninety-mile ordeal. "So Ragged Tetsu wants to go along," the senior smirked. "Be back here at four a.m."

Since it was already past one in the morning, Tesshu returned home to catch a few hours sleep. When he arrived at the senior's house promptly at four o'clock, it was pouring rain. Badly hung over, the blowhard senior was barely able to stand, let alone walk ninety miles in a rainstorm. "Then I'll go alone," Tesshu declared and took off. Eleven o'clock that night, Tesshu returned to the house, opened the entranceway door, and shouted, "I'm back!" When the startled senior came to answer the door, he found Tesshu standing in the entranceway, covered head to foot with mud. The three-inch-high teeth on Tesshu's wooden clogs, new that morning, were completely worn away.

There are other examples of Tesshu's dare-taking. Young swordsmen of his day liked to brag about how much they could eat and drink. An acquaintance boasted to Tesshu, "I ate thirty hard-boiled eggs at one sitting."

"Only thirty?" Tesshu raised his eyebrows. "You should be able to eat fifty. I can eat a hundred."

"Really?," the acquaintance challenged Tesshu. A hundred hard-boiled eggs were brought and Tesshu gulped them down in front of several witnesses. Tesshu returned home and vomited for the next three days.

On a similar dare (with similar results), Tesshu put away a hundred and eight large bean cakes. Tesshu once downed nine bottles of sake (each bottle contained about two quarts) in a drinking contest; a challenger consumed eleven, but he passed out—under the rules one had to return home under one's own power—and Tesshu was declared the winner.

Tesshu did, however, taste defeat at the hands of the "Sake Hero" Ikeda Tokutaro. The two of them downed seven gallons of sake one evening. The next morning, Tesshu, his head splitting, thought to himself, "If I have a hangover, Ikeda must be dead." When he arrived at Ikeda's home, Tesshu found Ikeda with a towel wrapped around his head and his wife massaging his back.

"Hung over?" Tesshu smiled.

"A little. How about you?"

"I'm fine," Tesshu lied.

"I bought two gallons of sake on the way home last night. There is a little left in that container over there. Help yourself."

For once, Tesshu did not respond.

Another time when Tesshu was drinking with companions, they told him of a horse so violent that no one could get near it, let alone ride it.

"What!" Tesshu exclaimed. "An animal that no man can control! That is ridiculous!"

"You try and ride it then," his friends countered.

"Let me at him," huffed Tesshu and off the group went to the stable.

Tesshu walked straight into the horse's stall, grabbed it by the tail, and started yanking. "Look out, you madman!" the others yelled as they headed for cover. To everyone's surprise, the animal no man could tame meekly followed Tesshu out of the stall and stood at bay in the middle of the stable. (When Tesshu told this tale to his disciples years later, he explained, "Animals confronted with determination greater than their own immediately submit. I knew that and was therefore able to control that horse. Also, I was quite drunk which made me even bolder than usual.")

Despite such reckless abandon, Tesshu had nothing to do with the many acts of terrorism committed by the more radical members of the sonno-joi movement. The group of which Tesshu was in charge was particularly rowdy. Their favorite pastimes were *tsuji-giri*, "cutting down passersby at the crossroads," and ransacking rich merchants' homes. In order to prevent such criminal acts, Tesshu would gather them together for a party every evening. After getting everyone sufficiently drunk, Tesshu would remove his clothes, dancing and singing ecstatically, urging the others to join in. Tesshu kept it up until the entire group was exhausted. All would collapse, sleeping soundly till dawn. If they did not have their clothes on, they could not carry their swords and cause trouble.

No matter how involved with political affairs, Tesshu never neglected his practice of zazen. Kiyokawa Hachiro, a prominent radical leader, complained, "You waste too much time doing zazen. When you sit, are you working for your lord? Are you serving the nation? The people?"

Tesshu replied with a question of his own: "Are you so sure that you yourself are really serving your lord, your country, and the people?"

"Of course I am," Hachiro shot back haughtily. "I serve them day and night."

"Excuse me for saying so," Tesshu told him politely, "but I don't think you are really serving anyone but yourself. Your servants at home are expected to serve you at all times without regard to their own comfort. They don't make it a 'principle' to serve you; they simply go quietly about their duty. If you overestimate the value of your service to the nation and keep account of every service you render, that is not service at all. You are merely doing those things for the sake of imagined rewards. Forget about yourself, keep your countrymen in your heart, and your mouth closed. Never boast of serving your country this way or that way—then you will be truly serving the fatherland." (Incidentally, Kiyokawa, an advocate of violent solutions to the nation's problems, was later assassinated by a rival group.)

In 1867, Tesshu joined the personal guard of Shogun Tokugawa Yoshinobu. The Shogunate, however, was in its death throes. On January 3, 1868, armed contingents led by Satsuma samurai seized the Tokugawa palace in Kyoto in the name of the new emperor Meiji, simultaneously declaring the Shogunate abolished.

A brief civil war ensued. The superior Imperial Forces beat back the loyalist troops' attempt to recapture Kyoto, soundly defeated them at Toba-Fushimi, and advanced rapidly on Edo, the last Tokugawa stronghold. Yoshinobu and his advisors met to discuss their next move. Most favored "waiting," that is to say, "put off a decision until the last possible minute." Tesshu, on the other hand, insisted on immediate action, saying, "All will be lost if we procrastinate." When asked what he had in mind, Tesshu offered to go and negotiate directly with Saigo Takamori, commander of the Imperial Forces. "That is too dangerous," the others protested. "You are certain to be killed before you can get anywhere near him."

Tesshu was not deterred. He obtained Yoshinobu's consent to negotiate in his name, stopped home to inform his wife he was leaving on an "errand," and then departed for Saigo's headquarters in Shizuoka. Even though Shizuoka was swarming with heavily armed sentries, Tesshu took the direct route, marching steadily and steadfastly in the middle of the road. He reached Saigo's camp without being challenged—only a hero or a fool could stride so confidently through enemy lines.

Tesshu told Saigo, in essence, "Continuance of this civil war will destroy the country. Further fighting must be avoided. Is slaughter of our countrymen the wish of the emperor?" Saigo consulted with his aides and returned with a proposal. The Imperial Forces would agree to peace if Tokugawa Yoshinobu would accept the following five conditions:

1. Surrender of Edo Castle
2. Evacuation of all troops from the compound
3. Surrender of all weapons
4. Surrender of all warships
5. Yoshinobu's exile to Bizen

Tesshu stated, "I can agree to all but one condition. I cannot accept the provision that Yoshinobu be exiled. His retainers could never acquiesce to such a needless affront."

"It is an imperial command!" Saigo said forcefully.

"Even so," Tesshu answered calmly, "I cannot agree to it."

"It is an imperial command!"

"Please put yourself in my position. I have sworn allegiance to my lord and must do everything in my power to maintain his honor. If our positions were reversed, what would you do?"

Saigo was silent for a time and then said, "I understand. I cannot give you a formal reply without discussing the matter with the other generals, but I will do my best. By the way, how did you get here from Edo?"

"I walked along the main highway," Tesshu said.

Slightly puzzled, Saigo asked him, "Didn't you see anything unusual on your way here?"

"Yes. The roads were lined with sentries. It was quite impressive."

After exchanging a few cups of sake, Saigo gave Tesshu a document allowing him safe passage back to Edo. On the way home, Tesshu ran across a groom leading a small group of horses. "Whose horses are those?" he asked the groom.

"They are a gift from my lord to the Imperial Forces."

"Well, I'm a member of the Imperial Forces now so let me have one," said Tesshu as he jumped on one of the horses and took off.

Tesshu got through the enemy lines without incident, but when he neared Edo his own sentries fired on him. Fortunately, Tesshu made it back safely, Saigo did not insist on Yoshinobu's exile, Edo castle was turned over peacefully to the Imperial Forces, and much bloodshed was avoided. Scattered fighting continued in the provinces for another year, but eventually the entire country was brought under Imperial control. Edo, renamed Tokyo, became capital city of the new Meiji government.

(There is some controversy surrounding the meeting between Saigo and Tesshu. Supporters of Katsu Kaishu claim that Tesshu was no more than a messenger who merely carried a letter from Kaishu to Saigo, and that the real negotiations took place in a later meeting between Kaishu and Saigo. It is clear, however, from Tesshu's own version and other sources that Tesshu conducted the initial negotiations as Yoshinobu's representative.)

While a few of Tokugawa Yoshinobu's closest retainers retired from public life together with their lord, many, like Tesshu, joined the new Meiji government. In 1869, Tesshu was assigned to Shizuoka to assist in the reorganization of that district's administration. Food, clothing, and shelter were in short supply and many had been displaced by the fighting. Tesshu worked tirelessly to reclaim and open new land for distribution to the impoverished residents. Tesshu also helped develop the Maki-no-hara tea groves which today produce sixty percent of Japan's tea. After serving in Shizuoka for two years, Tesshu was posted briefly to Ibaragi and Imari Prefectures. In 1872, Tesshu was appointed to the Imperial Household where he became Emperor Meiji's close confidant and most trusted aide.

Despite his heavy responsibilities as a statesman and the constant demands on his time, Tesshu was still able to devote himself wholeheartedly to his true work: perfection of the spirit through the practice and teaching of the Way. Like most of us today, Tesshu's duties prevented him from leisurely dabbling in religion and art. He was unable to "get away" from his many obligations, but that did not hinder him at all: public service, family life, and great enlightenment were not incompatible. Now on to the real story.

2

THE SWORD OF NO-SWORD

Known as "Ragged Tetsu," Tesshu had another nickname: "Demon Tetsu." Whatever Tesshu took up, no matter how minor, he gave it his all. Although Tesshu's father was not much of a martial artist, the Ono clan counted many illustrious swordsmen in its past, and Choemon was eager to have his energetic son follow in the footsteps of his ancestors. The boy was introduced to swordsmanship at age nine by the *Shinkage Ryu* master Kusumi Kantekisai, and thereafter never missed a day of practice. Upon the family's move to Taka-yama, Tesshu received instruction from Inoue Kiyotora, a highly regarded swordsman of the *Ono Itto Ryu*.

In Edo, Tesshu enrolled in the Kobukan, the national military institute, and made the rounds of the famous training halls (*dojo*) in the area. Tesshu, a massive six-footer with tremendous strength, became the scourge of Edo training halls. He once shattered a two-inch-thick wallboard in the Kobukan kendo hall with one of his thrusts. Several dojos prohibited Tesshu from making strikes to his opponent's *kote* (wrist protector) for fear of a broken arm. Tesshu always carried his training gear with him; whenever he heard the sound of bamboo swords he would rush in and request to participate. At joint training sessions, most swordsmen would take a breather following each contest. Not Tesshu—he kept his helmet on and faced one swordsman after another. His friends joked, "Demon

Tetsu likes swordsmanship better than eating or sleeping."

Regardless of the nature of their visit, callers to Tesshu's resi-
dence inevitably found themselves in his garden crossing swords
with their host. When deliverymen made their morning rounds,
Tesshu, naked save for his loincloth (*fundoshi*), would invite them to
strike with all their might on any part of his body. The deliverymen
naturally tired of bruising their knuckles on their strange customer's
rockhard frame and asked Tesshu's brother to intercede on their
behalf.

"But I'm simply conditioning my body," Tesshu explained. "We
samurai must be ready for anything."

"That may be true," his brother said, "but you are scaring away
all the deliverymen. How are you going to get provisions?"

"All right, all right!" Tesshu laughed. "Pass the word that there
will be no more early morning training."

During those first years in Edo, Tesshu engaged in thousands
upon thousands of contests with the best swordsmen of Japan. He
never relaxed his warrior's bearing, not even in the toilet or when
asleep. Accidentally awakened by a friend one night, Tesshu, who
slept with his practice sword, was on his feet in an instant, counter-
attacking.

One day, however, the confident twenty-eight-year-old demon
met his match in Asari Gimei (Yoshiaki), master swordsman of the
Nakanishi-ha Itto Ryu. As soon as Tesshu learned that this renowned
swordsman was in town, he applied for a contest. The arrange-
ments were made and the two swordsmen came together. The contest lasted half a day. Tesshu attacked furiously, but Asari turned
aside each blow, keeping Tesshu at bay the entire time. Finally, they
came together in a clinch, their swords locked at the handles. Tesshu
used his superior height and weight to knock Asari to the floor.

Asari got up and they faced each other in the middle of the hall.
"What do you think about this match?" Asari asked Tesshu.

"It was a tough fight, but luckily I was able to win," Tesshu replied proudly.

"No, I am the winner," Asari asserted.

"You are mistaken. I won," Tesshu maintained.

"Just before you knocked me down, I scored a clean strike against your chest protector."

"That's impossible. I didn't feel a thing."

"Check your chest protector."

Tesshu did so and discovered three broken bamboo strips on the protector. Tesshu, refusing to believe he had lost, shouted indignantly, "These marks were made by insects and I never noticed them before!"

Later that day, Tesshu's brother-in-law Deishu, a witness to the contest, visited Tesshu's home and told him, "You know, Asari was telling you the truth."

"Yes," Tesshu confessed. "I realize that myself."

As was the custom in those days, Tesshu became the disciple of the one who defeated him. Asari was even more intimidating in regular practice. The first time the two faced each other with wooden swords, Tesshu was unable to put Asari on the defensive. In fact, Asari, half Tesshu's size and twelve years older, repeatedly forced Tesshu all the way back to the wall of the training hall. Asari's *kiai* (spiritual force) was irresistible. Finally, Asari drove Tesshu right out of the dojo into the street, knocked him down, and unceremoniously slammed the door in his face.

Whenever Tesshu closed his eyes, he would see Asari standing before him like a mountain, bearing down on the bewildered trainee. Troubled by this constant vision, Tesshu redoubled his efforts, both in the training hall and on the meditation cushion. Zen master Ganno advised him, "If an opponent frightens or confuses you, it means you lack true insight. Solve the koan of 'Originally not one thing exists' (*honrai muichibutsu*) and nothing will obstruct you."

Even though Tesshu managed to solve this koan after ten years of contemplation, he still could not shake the perplexing apparition. Tesshu consulted with Tekisui, abbot of Tenryuji, who presented the swordsman with this koan taken from Tozan's Five Ranks:

> When two flashing swords meet there is
>   no place to escape;
> Move on coolly, like a lotus flower blooming
>   in the midst of a roaring fire,
> And forcefully pierce the Heavens!

(This is rank number four, mutual integration. A true practitioner moves without hesitation through the confusion and chaos of the sensual world, avoiding all duality.)

Every minute for the next three years, Tesshu butted his head against this koan. During breaks in conversation, Tesshu would cross two pipes, trying to figure out the problem; while eating, he put his chopsticks together like two swords. Tesshu always kept a pair of wooden swords near his bed. If a possible solution presented itself at night, Tesshu would jump out of bed and ask his wife to grab a sword and confront him.

In his forty-fifth year the many years of hard training and ceaseless introspection culminated in Tesshu's great enlightenment. On the morning of March 30, 1880, as Tesshu sat in zazen, the meaning of Tekisui's koan revealed itself. He lost all sense of time and space; Asari's threatening sword vanished.

> For years I forged my spirit through the
>   study of swordsmanship,
> Confronting every challenge steadfastly.
> The walls surrounding me suddenly crumbled;
> Like pure dew reflecting the world in crystal clarity, total
>   awakening has now come.

That same morning Tesshu went to Asari's dojo to test his awakening. As soon as Asari crossed swords with Tesshu, he knew his disciple had realized the state of "no-enemy." Asari withdrew his sword and declared, "You have arrived." It is said that after he officially designated Tesshu his successor as thirteenth Headmaster of the Nakanishi-ha Itto Ryu, Asari never picked up a sword again.

Shortly thereafter, Tesshu established the *Muto Ryu*. *Mu-to*, "no-sword," was not a new concept. Tesshu considered himself a restorer, rather than an innovator—his favorite quotation from the Confucian Analects was: "Do not make up your own teachings but cherish the ways of the ancients"—and his system (*Ryu*) was firmly based in the traditions of the past. Following his designation as the tenth Headmaster of the Ono Itto Ryu by Ono Nario, Tesshu henceforth referred to his school as the *Itto Shoden Muto Ryu*, "The No-Sword System of the Correct Transmission of Ito Ittosai."

Although Tesshu had a small makeshift dojo on his property, once he founded the Muto Ryu a larger training hall was needed. Tesshu used his retirement fund from the government to construct a hall he named the Shumpukan. The name refers to a poem by Bukko Kokushi, a thirteenth century Chinese priest who came to Japan to teach warrior Zen to the Kamakura Shoguns. When Bukko was still on the mainland, his temple was raided by fierce Mongol troops. As the soldiers rushed forward with their swords drawn, Bukko looked up calmly from his meditation and recited this poem:

> In heaven and earth no spot to hide;
> Bliss belongs to one who knows that things
>   are empty and that man too is nothing.
> Splendid indeed is the Mongol longsword
> Slashing the spring wind like a flash of lightning!

Not total barbarians, the Mongols were impressed enough by Bukko's composure to leave the priest unharmed.

"Spring wind" in Japanese is "*shumpu*." Tesshu's Shumpukan (*kan* means hall) was not merely a gym where one learned to hit others over the head with a stick; it was a holy "place of the Way" where the spirit was forged and awakening fostered.

> Using thought to analyze reality is illusion;
> If preoccupied with victory and defeat, all will be lost.
> The secret of swordsmanship?
> Lightning slashes the spring wind!

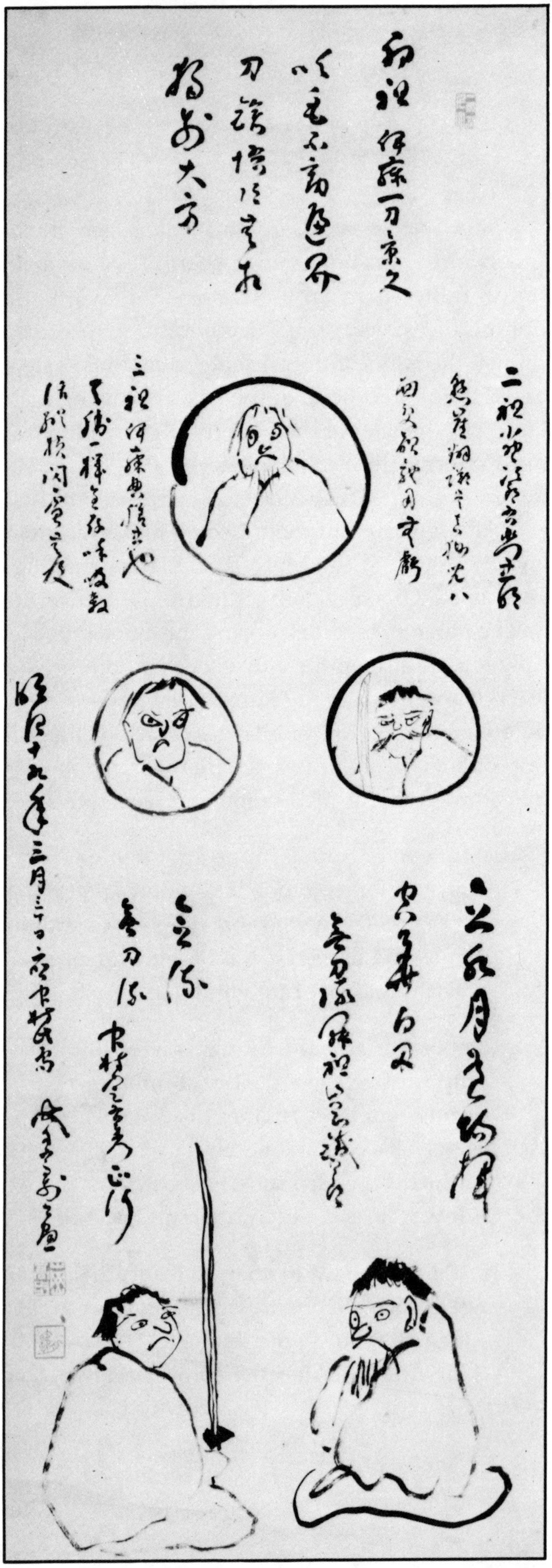

This delightful painting, dated March 30, 1886, depicts the Three Patriarchs of the Itto Ryu. In the center is the Founder Ito Ittosai Kagehisa. The inscription above him reads:

> His peerless sword of wisdom cut through
> the world of relativity.
> Enlightenment attained, form forgotten.
> Master of all, striding through the universe.

On the right is the Second Patriarch Ono Jiroemon Tadaaki. The verse above him says:

> Perched on a precipice, a true lion's son;
> Even when challenged from all directions
> his free-flowing power never diminished.

To the left is the Third Patriarch Ito Tenzen Tadanari. His verse reads:

> A special method of attaining heavenly victory by
> being in harmony with all things;
> Life, death, length, and breadth: not a spark of discord.

Beneath the Three Patriarchs, Tesshu has drawn himself on the right explaining about the patriarchs to his disciple, Mr. Nakamura, on the left. Above Tesshu is the inscription:

> Standing in the dojo of suigetsu
> Slashing at the flowers of emptiness.

This is Tesshu's version of the Zen saying, "Sitting on the dojo of suigetsu, practicing myriad forms of empty flowers." Both Buddhas and worldlings see flowers of emptiness, but those who are enlightened know that they are false while those who are deluded think that they are real.

At the Shumpukan, Tesshu placed little emphasis on complicated explanations or rational analysis of technique. He rarely corrected his trainees' hand or foot work. Unlike other schools of swordsmanship where trainees were told, "If your opponent assumes such-and-such a stance, take such-and-such a stance in response," new Muto Ryu swordsmen were instructed to devote themselves exclusively to *uchi-komi* for at least three years. *Uchi-komi* is "attack training," repeated straight blows to the opponent's *men* (top of the head). The important element was never to retreat or hesitate; swordsmen must keep up the attack until they drop. It was not that Tesshu disregarded technique; forbearance can be developed no other way. When students complained of a lack of progress after a year's training, Tesshu thundered, "You've just begun!" Pointing to his abdomen, he continued, "You must experience swordsmanship here!"

Three years of uchi-komi training had many benefits: the body naturally became hardened; one developed strong arms, a powerful grip, sharp vision, and stable hips; one's movement gradually became free-flowing, characterized by forceful blows and sweeping attacks; unconcerned with winning and losing, totally absorbed in the moment at hand, one attained presence of mind. (Critics of this system referred to Muto Ryu training as "wood-chopping.")

For advanced swordsmen, Tesshu had more severe forms of training. Tesshu initiated a special method he termed *seigan*. "Seigan" is a Buddhist term meaning "vow," such as Shakyamuni's vow to attain enlightenment, or a Bodhisattva's vow to save all sentient beings. In this instance, it was a vow to challenge death in order to attain the ultimate principles of swordsmanship.

There were three kinds of seigan. The first seigan was generally preceded by a 1,000-consecutive-day practice period. On the final day of the period, the candidate was required to engage in a two-hundred-contest seigan with the other swordsmen in the dojo. With the exception of a brief pause for a lunch of rice gruel and pickled plums, the swordsman stood continuously (i.e., *tachi-kiri*, as seigan was also known), facing fresh opponents one after the other. The

Shoki, the popular demon-queller of folk-art, is depicted here as a master swordsman.

> Demons stay away!
> Shoki is on guard in emptiness!

Swordsmen who are totally awake stand in emptiness (*ku*), without the slightest attachment to things and events. The "Book of Emptiness," the last of Musashi's *Five Rings,* states that one is a master of the Way when one is "free of confusion, the clouds of illusion have vanished, and true emptiness is known."

This *kappa*, a fantastic water sprite of great strength and fighting spirit, is a formidable foe in a wrestling match. Tesshu gives us this advice:

> Don't hold back,
> Trying to protect your ass;
> As soon as an
> Opening appears,
> Seize it!

(Kappas supposedly like to snatch their opponent's liver through the anus.)

contests ran from early in the morning until two hundred were completed some time in the afternoon.

Successful candidates were eligible, after further training, for the second seigan: six hundred matches over a three-day period, following the same format as the first seigan.

The supreme test was the third seigan, a seven-day, one-thousand-four-hundred-contest marathon which taxed the outer limits of the swordsman's physical and spiritual endurance. Tesshu wrote:

> Swordsmanship should lead to the heart of things where one can directly confront life and death. Recently, swordsmanship has become a mere pastime with no bearing on matters of importance. In order to counter this tendency, I have instituted a one-week, one-thousand-four-hundred-match training session. Initially, the swordsman will find the contests similar to regular training; however, as the number of consecutive matches piles up, it will assume the dimensions of a fight to the finish—one must rely on spiritual strength. This is real swordsmanship. If single-minded determination is absent, one will never advance regardless of the years spent in training. Thus I have established this special method of training to test the resolve of my swordsmen. Fortify your spirit and throw yourselves into this practice!

Two accounts remain of swordsmen who underwent seigan:

Kagawa Zenjiro was the first candidate: "On day one, the matches began at 6:00 a.m. Ten opponents took turns facing me and except for a short lunch break, I didn't sit down or remove my training gear until I completed the two hundred contests around 6:00 that evening. It was demanding, but I was in reasonably good condition. However, one of my fellow trainees visited my home later to relay this message from Tesshu Sensei: "You are slacking off. You must try harder."

"The second day, I resolved to give it my all. Tesshu, too, had instructed my opponents to show no mercy. By mid-afternoon I was suffering greatly from fatigue. I somehow completed the required number of matches and limped home. My legs were so badly swollen I was unable to get up to go to the toilet. Near the end of the third day, I was staggering around the dojo, barely able to stand.

Just then a former trainee entered the hall to be one of my opponents. A sneaky, ill-mannered lout, notorious for his unfair tactics, he liked nothing better than to injure his opponents seriously. My pain and weariness vanished; I focused entirely on my devious opponent. Even if he smashed my skull, he too would fall. Raising my sword high above my head I was about to leap across the dojo to meet him when Tesshu suddenly called out, 'Excellent! Excellent! Stop now!' Puzzled because I had not finished the quota of matches, Tesshu told me not to worry and to return home. I neither ate nor slept that night. My wife helped me to my feet the next morning. It was raining, but I couldn't raise my arms to hold an umbrella so she threw a blanket around me. I went to the training hall certain this would be my last day on earth—I was determined to die rather than not complete the seigan. When I arrived at the dojo, Tesshu was waiting for me. 'Ready to continue?' he asked. 'Yes,' I immediately replied. To my surprise, Tesshu ordered me to stop, and had the other trainees complete the remainder of the session." Because Kagawa had realized the "sword of no-sword" Tesshu had no need to test him further.

Yanagita Ganjiro completed the two-hundred-match seigan on the final day of his thousand-day training period. He then practiced five hundred more days in a row and undertook the three-day, six-hundred-match seigan. Blows received from the short, thick Muto Ryu bamboo sword (shinai) were extremely painful. Yanagita recalled: "After the first day my head was full of lumps and my body covered with bruises, but I did not feel weak. On the second day I began to suffer. I thought I would have to give up halfway. I managed to continue and near the end of the day I experienced 'selflessness'—I naturally blended with my opponent and moved in unhindered freedom. Although my spirit was strong, my body was weak. My urine was dark red and I had no appetite. Nevertheless, I passed the final day's contests with a clear mind; I felt as if I was floating among the clouds."

Tesshu was not impressed with such hardship. He told his disciples: "When I was twenty-four I participated in a joint training session and engaged in one thousand four hundred matches over a seven-day period. I do not remember feeling tired or being in pain. There is victory and defeat in swordsmanship, but forging the spirit is far more important. What is the secret? The mind has no limits. Use such a mind when facing your opponents, incorporate it in your movements, and you will never tire regardless of how many days and how many contests you have. Study this and practice harder!"

Unfortunately, no firsthand accounts survive by the two swordsmen who completed the seven-day seigan: Kominami Yasutomo and Sano (Tojo) Jisaburo. (Sano's "memorial" seven-day seigan took place after Tesshu's death.) According to Shumpukan records, eight swordsmen successfully completed a one-day, two-hundred-match seigan. Ogura Tetsuju and Yanagita Ganjiro made the one-thousand-day practice that included a one-day seigan. Yanagita also completed a three-day seigan as did Kagawa Zenjiro. Two swordsmen, Kominami Yasutomo and Sano Jisaburo, underwent all three seigan: one-, three-, and seven-day. Another swordsman made a one-day *kata* seigan consisting of 2,750 movements. Successful completion of a seigan was accompanied by presentation of certificates, catalogs of techniques, and memorial training gear. However, the records are not clear on this point and it appears that the system was not uniformly applied.

Depth of spirit alone is not enough; it must be combined with technical prowess to create true swordsmanship. To foster proper technique, Tesshu had his trainees follow the classical kata of the Itto Ryu. When mastered, "kata," set forms that cover the entire range of techniques, enable a swordsman to adjust to any contingency. Unlike the contrived, artificially constructed kata of many other schools, Muto Ryu kata are all derived from actual combat conditions. There are fifty basic Muto Ryu kata—to perform the entire sequence requires nearly thirty minutes—plus a series of highly advanced kata. Again, emphasis is placed on the fundamentals: at least three years should be spent on perfecting the first five kata.

Regular practice in the Shumpukan ran from 6:00 to 9:00 in the morning. The live-in disciples rose at 4:00 to clean the grounds, sweep the training hall, and prepare the equipment. By 6:00, seventy to eighty swordsmen had gathered. Tesshu would circle the dojo, sometimes letting his disciples strike his helmet, sometimes countering in a flash and flipping them to the ground. There were no lengthy explanations—the only admonition was "Train harder! Train harder!"

Tesshu developed a kind of sixth sense, frequently surprising his disciples by telling them exactly what they were thinking. When asked about this "magic power," Tesshu told them: "It is nothing out of the ordinary. If your mind is empty, it reflects the 'distortions' and shadows' present in others' minds. In swordsmanship no-mind allows us to see the perfect place to strike; in daily life it enables us to see into another's heart."

Although Tesshu headed the Muto Ryu for only eight years, over four hundred students enrolled, including some of the most talented and eccentric swordsmen of Japan.

Even though Hasegawa Unhachiro, the senior Muto Ryu student, was in his seventies, he was the only swordsman who could more or less hold his own against Tesshu, always putting up strong resistance before going down to defeat. Extremely uncoordinated— throughout his life he could never swing a sword perfectly straight— Hasegawa exemplied Tesshu's favorite saying: "Unified in spirit, what cannot be accomplished?"

Tesshu got Hasegawa a job at the Imperial Palace as a guard. On payday, Hasegawa would buy a huge keg of sake, pleasantly tapping it every evening until the next pay envelope was due. Hasegawa passed from this world in a most suitable fashion. Gravely ill with cholera, Hasegawa leaped out of bed, grabbed his sword, and started swinging it furiously when Tesshu came to visit him. "Don't worry, Sensei," Hasegawa assured Tesshu. "I'm still fine." As soon as Tesshu departed, Hasegawa changed his mind, announced to those present, "I'm dying now," and keeled over.

When Nakajo Kinnosuke, an old acquaintance of Tesshu, heard that his younger colleague had established a new school of swordsmanship he went to investigate. Tesshu told his former supervisor, "If Miyamoto Musashi himself were to come back to challenge me, I wouldn't be defeated."

Nakajo was skeptical. "Are you serious? Let me have a match with you." When they crossed swords Nakajo was overwhelmed; he threw down his sword and declared, "In all my years of swordsmanship I've never witnessed anything like this."

Tesshu said, "It has taken me forty years to reach this level. I was much too hotheaded in my youth to master swordsmanship." Thus convinced, Nakajo enrolled in the Muto Ryu.

There is another version of this encounter. In those days a match would continue until one of the parties submitted by saying, "I give up" (*maitta* or *mairimashita*). After coming together, Tesshu knocked Nakajo down with a blow, but the older swordsman refused to concede defeat to his junior. Reluctantly, Tesshu kept up the attack and Nakajo eventually passed out. Later, Nakajo came to and returned home in a daze. Halfway there, Nakajo suddenly recalled what had occurred; he went back to Tesshu's house, opened the door, and shouted, "I give up!"

Murakami Masatada was another longtime acquaintance who also became a disciple. Murakami was famous, among other things, for calming a panicky crowd in a highly unusual, albeit effective, manner. Wood and paper Japanese houses catch, and spread, fire easily. During one particularly large conflagration in Tokyo, the townspeople rushed to a nearby bridge to escape. Unbeknownst to the people in the rear, the bridge, set aflame by debris from the main fire, had collapsed. Despite cries of "Stop shoving! The bridge is out!" those in front were being crushed and pushed into the river by the surge of the frantic crowd. Murakami, who was present at the scene, drew his sword and cut down several men in the center of the crowd while yelling, "I'll kill you all! I'll kill you all!" Terrified, the throng scattered along the side of the river (and thus to safety) to flee the madman. This type of crowd control can hardly be recommended as standard procedure, but the sacrifice of a few led to the salvation of many.

Like many other samurai who lost their source of livelihood when the feudal system was abolished, Murakami was constantly short of funds. Although both his brother-in-law Kaishu and his teacher Tesshu provided Murakami with stipends, he was always pestering them for more. Murakami was able to intimidate the aged Kaishu, but Tesshu got fed up and ordered him to live within his means. Murakami, intoxicated at the time, got abusive and challenged Tesshu to a fight with real swords. "Anytime you are ready," Tesshu shot back. "I'll be waiting."

Tesshu took his wooden sword (even when his opponent was armed with a live blade, Tesshu generally used a wooden sword) and sat down to read until Murakami returned. When Murakami, now sober, sheepishly begged Tesshu's forgiveness, Tesshu sprang up and began chasing him through the house. The other disciples were amazed to see Tesshu, who was noted for his extraordinarily even temper, with such a ferocious expression. Tesshu cornered Murakami, making him promise never to bother anyone again about money. While the disciples had never seen a more terrifying countenance than Tesshu's, they never saw a face paler than Murakami's.

Murakami was quite a character. As skilled with a shamisen as with a sword, he was in big demand at banquets as a reciter of popular ballads. Whenever a seigan was held at the Shumpukan, Murakami would lead a steady refrain of "Kill the bastard!"

On the day of Tesshu's funeral, Murakami was taken into protective custody for fear he would commit *seppuku* (ritual suicide). Murakami was never the same after Tesshu's death, leading an aimless existence until his own death some years later.

Years before, a gang of Tesshu's rivals selected Matsuoka Yorozu, a specialist in tsuji-giri (street-fighting), to assassinate the young ronin leader. Under the pretext of engaging in a regular bamboo-sword contest, Matsuoka visited Tesshu's dojo.

"If it is not a contest with live blades," Matsuoka informed Tesshu, "I cannot get in the proper frame of mind. Let's use real swords."

Tesshu agreed and they drew their blades. Matsuoka could not detect the slightest opening in Tesshu's defenses; on the contrary, it was Matsuoka who was in danger. Matsuoka was forced to withdraw his sword and concede defeat. As was his custom, Tesshu invited his once life-threatening opponent to share a drink. Matsuoka, however, was still scheming. "If I don't accomplish my mission, how can I face my fellow conspirators?"

At the restaurant, Matsuoka told Tesshu, "Actually, I'm better at jujutsu than swordfighting. Let me try a hold on you." Matsuda positioned himself behind Tesshu and applied a choke hold, fully intending to break Tesshu's neck. Tesshu escaped from the hold, held Matsuoka down with one hand, handed him a sake cup, and, without a trace of anger in his voice, said, "Drink this."

When Matsuoka confessed the true purpose of his visit, Tesshu told him to forget about it. Matsuoka was eager to join Tesshu's group, but before giving his assent, Tesshu extracted one promise. If either one of them missed a single day of training, the other could hit the negligent swordsman over the head with a wooden sword.

Rain or shine, Matsuoka appeared at the training hall. One midwinter day, however, he failed to show up. That evening Tesshu strolled over to Matsuoka's place and found him lying in bed stricken by food poisoning.

"What! You are still alive!" Tesshu scolded him. "Why didn't you come to the dojo? Did you forget our pledge?"

Later that night, there was a knock on Tesshu's door. Matsuoka, clad in his bedclothes, handed Tesshu a wooden sword and pleaded, "Kill me."

"You are not worth killing," sneered Tesshu as he slammed the door.

Matsuoka stood in the deep snow begging Tesshu to finish him off until Tesshu sent out a couple of disciples to quiet him down and take him home.

Tesshu had his hands full with Matsuoka, one of his "Three Crazies" (the other two were Murakami and Nakano Nobunari). Even after Matsuoka became Tesshu's disciple, he continued tsuji-giri whenever his teacher's back was turned.

One evening when the two were out together, Tesshu stopped to use the public toilet. In the meantime, Matsuoka disappeared. Following a brief search, Tesshu found him pointing his sword at a tall samurai, daring the man to fight. After angrily yanking Matsuoka back by the collar, Tesshu apologized to the other samurai for his companion's unruly behavior. The samurai, standing calmly with his arms folded, said, "It was nothing," and then fainted dead away.

On another occasion, without Tesshu's knowledge and for reasons clear to only himself, Matsuoka went to assassinate the minister Iwakura Tonomi. Iwakura dissuaded Matsuoka from that course of action, giving him instead a firm lecture on public responsibility. In his inimitable manner, Matsuoka totally misinterpreted Iwakura's remarks, and decided to sacrifice himself for the nation. With a surprising lack of skill for an expert swordsman, Matsuoka did such a poor job of cutting his throat that he remained conscious until Tesshu was summoned.

As soon as Tesshu entered the room, Matsuoka proclaimed grandly, "Today I'm sacrificing myself for the sake of the nation."

"You idiot!" Tesshu exploded. "What would the nation do with a piece of shit like you! I'm getting out of here right now!"

Matsuoka recovered from this hapless attempt at self-sacrifice, but his past ultimately caught up with him. Tormented by the vengeful spirits of the many souls he had mercilessly cut down, Matsuoka died in alcoholic misery.

Nakano Nobunari, the third "Crazy," liked to say, "Tesshu Sensei is holding my life in his hands." Nakano's lord was killed during the civil war and he went to Tesshu for advice.

"Your master has fallen in battle," Tesshu counseled. "In order not to sully his memory, you should commit seppuku and follow him into death."

Nakano was not too keen on the suggestion, but Tesshu insisted that there was no honorable alternative. Nakano settled himself in correct posture, collected his thoughts, and was about to plunge his dagger into his abdomen when Tesshu yelled, "Wait! Since you have made the necessary preparations, I'll hold your life in trust for a while."

The two pillars of the Shumpukan were Kominami Yasutomo and Kagawa Zenjiro. Kominami, one of two swordsmen to complete all three seigan, went blind in his old age. Even then, it is said, he could execute the Muto Ryu kata with unerring accuracy.

Of all Tesshu's immediate disciples, Kagawa probably had the greatest influence on the development of modern kendo. In his capacity as head instructor of the National Police Academy, Kagawa taught throughout Japan and his top student, Ishikawa Ryuzo, trained several of the twentieth century's outstanding swordsmen. One of the author's teachers, now deceased, remembered well his encounter with Kagawa Sensei:

> Our instructor, Ishikawa Sensei, was a disciple of Kagawa Sensei, so when Kagawa Sensei was in the area, we invited him to give a lesson at our high school. Forty-five of us lined up to take turns facing him. Despite the fact that Kagawa Sensei was near seventy years old, one minute apiece was all the pounding we could take—his blows staggered us. After finishing with us, he took on Ishikawa Sensei. Both of them were over six feet tall, but Ishikawa Sensei was quite a bit heavier. As Ishikawa Sensei rushed forward to strike, Kagawa Sensei slipped his sword underneath our teacher's hands, twisted sharply, and threw Ishikawa Sensei across the floor. Ishikawa Sensei was on his feet in an instant to continue his assault. Again he hit the deck. Generally, even the finest swordsmen can do little more than unbalance their opponents. Kagawa Sensei, however, was actually flipping Ishikawa Sensei through the air. Finally, Ishikawa Sensei crashed to the floor unable to move any further. While we helped our teacher up, Kagawa Sensei calmly removed his training gear as if nothing

unusual had occurred. I never saw anything like it before or since; one shudders to think of what training was like in the heyday of the Shumpukan.

Yanagita Ganjiro, veteran of 1,500 straight days of training and the one- and three- day seigan, was a highly regarded kendo instructor at Tohoku University in Sendai and author of the standard Meiji-era textbook, *Kendo Kyohan*.

At first, Ogura Tetsuju (then known as Watanabe Isaburo) felt out of place at the Shumpukan. Tetsuju was a student of the Chinese classics, and the hectic life of a live-in disciple left little time for reading. Ogura temporarily abandoned his practice at the Shumpukan to study at other academies, but he soon realized that the best education he could ever receive was at Tesshu's training hall. Tesshu agreed to readmit Ogura and told him to fetch a signboard. On it Tesshu wrote: "Watanabe Isaburo vows to complete 1,000 days of training." Tesshu then had the signboard posted in the dojo.

The senior disciples gave the bookworm Ogura an especially hard time, saving their most powerful whacks for the upstart. Nevertheless, Ogura completed the full term, including the one-day seigan on the final day. Eventually, though, Ogura abandoned swordsmanship for a life of scholarship and Zen training. Later, Ogura founded the *Ichikukai Dojo* in Tokyo where several prominent twentieth century martial artists learned Zen and *misogi* exercises.

Sano Jisaburo, the only other swordsman to complete all three seigan, was Ogura's diametrical opposite. Son of a poverty-stricken tofu seller in Osaka, Sano was largely illiterate and earned his living as a construction worker. Kendo was his life; every minute outside work was spent in the dojo. Over the years, Sano became a respected instructor and died, of a stroke, in the midst of a training session.

Playboy swordsman Suzuki Yuso (Kancho) was one of the scoundrels responsible for forgeries of Tesshu's calligraphy. A skilled calligrapher, Suzuki could produce nearly perfect copies of his teacher's works. Whenever he was out of money, Suzuki would brush a score of "Yamaoka Tesshu" calligraphies and sell them in outlying districts. Flush, he would then squander every yen in the red-light district. One day, as Tesshu was walking past an art dealer's shop, he noticed a "Tesshu" calligraphy hanging in the window. He brought the forgery home, called in Suzuki, and bawled him out. "You wrote this, didn't you? A real disciple of mine would never do such a thing!" (Suzuki was not the only culprit in the household. Sad to say, there is good evidence that, after Tesshu's death, his son Naoki used his father's seals on his own pieces.)

Grief-stricken when Tesshu died, Suzuki shaved his head, built a small hut near his Master's grave and attended it day and night for three years. For the convenience of the many pilgrims who visited the grave, Suzuki sold incense and flowers. He did not use a single yen of that money, so a sizable amount accumulated. On the third anniversary of Tesshu's death, Suzuki used the money to throw a huge bash in memory of his teacher. Following the three years of mourning, Suzuki returned to society, eventually becoming a very wealthy businessman.

In addition to regular swordsmen, several important government officials trained at the Shumpukan, not so much to master kendo as to deepen and broaden the spirit. These officials included the distinguished governors, Koteda Yasusada and Kitagaki Kunimichi, and the noted judge, Kawamura Yoshimasu.

Among the colorful swordsmen who paid courtesy calls on Tesshu were "Asaemon the Headsman" and the "Terror of Edo." Asaemon was one of the official executioners for the old military regime. During his tenure, he lopped off well over two thousand heads. Tesshu asked him, "You saw many people in their extremity. Did you ever witness anything extraordinary?"

"Only once," Asaemon replied. "I was scheduled to execute the bandit Nezumi Kozo [the Japanese Robin Hood] and his lover, the courtesan Hanacho. Hanacho was first. She refused the blindfold and awaited the slash of the blade with perfect composure. When I raised my sword to deliver the judgment, my hands froze. I lowered the blade and tried again. For the first time in a thousand attempts, I vacillated. Finally, I took a deep breath, determined to make myself worthy of taking Hanacho's head. This time I followed through. Nezumi Kozo was next. He too strode resolutely up to the execution site and refused the blindfold: 'Please strike at once.' Again, I had the greatest difficulty overcoming my condemned prisoner's superior spiritual force, succeeding only on the third attempt."

"I see," mused Tesshu. "Their hearts were pure and their consciences clear. Such a death is worthy of the noblest samurai."

Tesshu said to the "Terror of Edo," recently released from a long prison term, "I've heard that you had more than thirty sword fights. Where did you study swordsmanship?"

"I'm almost entirely self-taught and learned all of my tactics on the street," the Terror replied.

"How were you able to remain undefeated?"

"As soon as the challenge was made, I maneuvered close enough to feel the tip of my opponent's blade. If he was holding the sword stiffly, I knew I had him—one fell swoop and he would be finished. If, on the other hand, the sword was held flexibly with a steady projection of ki, I took no chances—I threw my sword right at him and ran away. That's how I remained undefeated."

There were some uninvited guests. A group of Saigo Takamori's supporters in Tokyo decided to take revenge on Tesshu, who, they felt, was partly responsible for their leader's defeat in the ill-fated rebellion of 1877. However, like all previous assassins, they were thwarted by Tesshu's indomitable physical and spiritual presence. During their "visit" to Tesshu's home, a conspirator named Shimada said darkly, "It's difficult to kill someone, isn't it?"

"Not at all," Tesshu remarked. "It's only difficult if you want to keep yourself alive." After the group left, Tesshu regretted his statement: "That fellow Shimada misunderstood me. He is up to no good." The following day Shimada cut down the foreign minister, Okubo Toshimichi, Saigo's chief antagonist in the Meiji government.

Tesshu had some memorable contests with several of the top masters of the day. A swordsman named Takayama stormed the Tokyo Police Academy Dojo and defeated thirty senior instructors in a row. Later, when he challenged Tesshu, he launched his trademark attack, but to no avail; Tesshu drove him straight back and sat him down in a chair in the vestibule of the training hall.

Tesshu occasionally gave formal demonstrations before the emperor. During such a contest with Watanabe Noburo, one of Tesshu's more worthy opponents, the swordplay was rather subtle and the emperor missed Tesshu's decisive score.

"If we use live blades," Tesshu said with perhaps a certain amount of sarcasm, "Your Majesty will be able to see when a point is scored."

"Isn't that dangerous?"

"No," Tesshu assured him. "A slight cut will draw blood and Your Eminence will get a clear view of the action."

The emperor declined.

Even most Japanese researchers are unaware of Tesshu's contest with the celebrated Sakakibara Kenkichi, fourteenth Headmaster of the Jikishinkage Ryu. After bowing to each other, both masters lifted their swords over their heads to assume *jodan-kamae*. Glaring like tigers, breathing from the deepest part of their abdomens, neither moved an inch. Sweat poured off their bodies and, in a few minutes, their uniforms were soaking wet. For more than forty minutes the standoff continued. Suddenly, both masters sheathed their swords, bowed deeply, and the match was over. None of the disciples present were able to discern the victor; the consensus was that because neither master could perceive the slightest opening in the other's defenses it was a draw. However, Tesshu rarely made the first move in a contest while Sakakibara was noted for his normally irresistible initiatory attack. Thus, it is more likely that Sakakibara was the one who was stymied.

Tesshu used his head to win one battle. When Ogusa Takijiro, one of Tesshu's commanders in the old days, learned of the Muto Ryu he vowed to teach his brash subordinate a lesson.

"Have you no shame?" Ogusa demanded as he stormed into Tesshu's room. "How dare you start your own school of swordsmanship! Take this!" As Ogusa pounded Tesshu's head with his fists, Tesshu calmly received the blows, making no effort to defend himself. Ogusa tired of punching Tesshu's face and left in a huff. When asked the reason for his behavior, Tesshu explained, "It is essential to harden our bodies and this incident was simply another form of training. It was a contest of wills, matching the pain in my head with the pain in Ogusa's hands. Since he was the one who gave up, I am the winner." Ogusa evidently thought so too because he later made a formal apology.

Tesshu's sword was the *katsujin-ken*, the blade that protects and fosters life. Although Tesshu never took another's life, he was ready to give up his own at any time. In the days prior to the Meiji Restoration, Tesshu was once walking through a forest when he met a hunter carrying a rifle. "Even the most skillful swordsman is no match for a gun," the hunter remarked as he pointed his rifle toward Tesshu. Without a second's hesitation, Tesshu drew his sword and rushed straight for the hunter. The startled hunter dropped his gun and ran off in confusion. The hunter, afraid of death, could not avoid defeat regardless of how well he was armed; Tesshu, willing to lose his life without regret, could not lose.

The life-giving sword has many aspects; on occasion it too can cut deeply. Usui, one of Tesshu's young trainees, was in constant torment. When he was eight years old, his parents had been ruthlessly murdered in their sleep by assassins. The boy swore some day to revenge his parents' deaths, and after he enrolled in the Shumpukan, he sought Tesshu's counsel.

"A lot of terrible things occurred in those days. Now that a new order has been established, it is best to put it out of your mind."

"I can't," Usui sobbed. "My heart will never be at rest until my parents are avenged."

"Then settle the matter," Tesshu told him.

Usui's target was a blackguard named Ise, the one who ordered the murder of his parents. Usui planned an attack, but held back because Ise was accompanied by bodyguards. (Ise had many enemies and never travelled alone.) When Tesshu heard about Usui's abortive attempt he exploded. "How can you be concerned with your personal safety when your parents' honor is at stake? You are a sniveling coward!" The next time Usui met up with his nemesis there was no reserve, and the vendetta was settled. (Largely through Tesshu's intercession Usui escaped execution, receiving instead a relatively light ten-year sentence.)

To Tesshu, the prime requisite of a swordsman is unyielding determination. When a friend asked for the secret of swordsmanship, Tesshu instructed him to seek the guidance of the Asakusa Kannon. The friend paid a visit to the temple housing that image, but received no revelation. Dejected, he was about to return home when he noticed the calligraphy board hanging above the statue. It read: "Giver of Fearlessness."

New entrants to the Shumpukan were told: "The purpose of Muto Ryu swordsmanship is not to fight to defeat others in contests; training in my dojo is to foster enlightenment, and for this you must be willing to risk your life. Attack me any way you wish. Do not hold back!" After knocking the novice to the floor, generally with a dynamic thrust, Tesshu would shout, "Get up and come at me again!" This would continue until the candidate dropped from exhaustion. Tesshu might keep up such treatment for a week in order to test the determination of the prospective trainee. Technical ability did not matter at all; if the candidate's spirit was strong, he was selected for admittance. Tesshu wrote, "If single-minded determination is absent, one will never advance regardless of the years in training . . . technique has its place, but spiritual forging is far more important."

Tesshu insisted that no-sword swordsmanship was ultimately pure spirit. Near the end of his life, Tesshu's movements were extraordinarily supple and he could defeat an opponent without even touching him. Students had sore spots on the places where Tesshu had merely pointed his sword at their bodies.

A week before his death, Tesshu called all his trainees together for a final practice session. Tesshu told them, "I'm dying. My physical strength is gone. I am barely able to stand. Not a trace of competitiveness remains. I'll now prove to you all that Muto Ryu swordsmanship is a thing of the spirit. If any of you display the slightest reserve today, the Muto Ryu will perish with my death."

Sano was the first to attack. Without regard for Tesshu's terminal illness, Sano charged forward. Just as he was about to bring his sword down with all his might, a tremendous force spun him around. Upon recovery, he cut loose with a two-handed thrust; in the twinkling of a eye, Sano was crushed to the floor. Seven or eight disciples came forward and all went flying in the same fashion. "This is the sword of no-sword."

The day before his death, Tesshu asked why the customary sounds were not rising from the dojo. The senior disciples, he was informed, had decided among themselves to call off the practice in order to be by Tesshu's side in his last hours. "What!" Tesshu thundered. "The best way to honor me and the Muto Ryu is to get in that hall right now and practice your hearts out!"

Although Tesshu awarded a number of certificates to various disciples, it appears that only two swordsmen received *menkyo-kaiden* teaching licenses, Hasegawa Unhachiro (awarded posthumously) and Kagawa Zenjiro. Since one of Tesshu's treasured swords and the Shumpukan files passed to Kagawa, he is commonly reckoned as the second Headmaster of the Muto Ryu. Kagawa's top disciple was Ishikawa Ryuzo who, in turn, instructed the three main Muto Ryu exponents of the twentieth century: Navy Chief of Staff Kusajika Ryunozuke, Chief Justice Ishida Kazuto, and Dr. Murakami Yasumasa. Murakami Sensei, the only surviving member of the three, currently heads the Muto Ryu and maintains the *Shum-*

pukan Bunko (Library) which preserves many of the original records.

The techniques and training methods of the Muto Ryu were never widespread—today, for example, there are no more than fifteen Muto Ryu swordsmen—and critics, then and now, say its methods are too severe and its principles too deep for wide application. That may well be: Tesshu was never interested in popularizing the Way of the Sword as a sport or pastime. To Tesshu, one good swordsman was worth 10,000 mediocre trainees.

Murakami Yasumasa Sensei, current headmaster of the Muto Ryu, demonstrating a kata with a disciple during a memorial service for Tesshu held at Zensho-an. Omori Sogen Roshi, founder of the Tesshu Society, looks on.

Numbers two, three, and four
of the Ten Ox-Herding Pictures,
a common theme of Zen artists.
Top, "Finding traces of the ox";
middle, "Seeing the ox"; and,
bottom, "Catching the ox." In
other words, a practitioner gets
a hint, then a glimpse, and then
a tentative hold on the elusive
reality of Zen.

3

GREAT ENLIGHTENMENT

"As a samurai, I must strengthen my character; as a human being, I must perfect my spirit." For Tesshu, this meant swordsmanship during the day and zazen at night. No matter how exhausted he was or how deeply involved with political affairs, Tesshu passed most of each night in meditation. Tesshu's chief inspiration was Daito Kokushi's "Final Admonitions":

> All of you who have come to this mountain! Do not forget that you are here for the sake of the Way, not for the sake of clothing and food. If you have shoulders, you will not lack clothes; if you have a mouth, you will not lack food. Direct yourselves, throughout all the hours of the day, to knowing the unknowable. From start to finish, investigate all things in detail. Time flies like an arrow so be careful not to waste energy on trivial matters. Be attentive! Be attentive!
>
> After this old monk completes his pilgrimage, some of you may preside over grand temples with magnificent buildings and huge libraries adorned with gold and silver, and have many ardent followers. Others may devote themselves to sutra study, esoteric chants, continual meditation, and strict observation of the precepts. Whatever the course of action, if one's mind is not set on the marvelous, untransmittable Way of the Buddhas and Patriarchs, causality is negated and the teaching collapses. Such people are devils and can never be my true heirs. The one who tends to his own affairs and clarifies his own nature, even though he may be residing far in the country, subsisting on wild vege-

tables and living in a thatched hut, encounters my tradition daily and receives my teaching with gratitude. Who can take this lightly? Work harder! Work harder!

Regarding Tesshu's practice of Zen, "Demon Tetsu" and "Ragged Tetsu" shared the stage. As poverty-stricken newlyweds, Tesshu and his wife were obliged to live in an old tumbledown house. Mice considered the building their private playground and ran wild through the place. However, once Tesshu began zazen, the mice would scatter and not a sound could be heard from them. When his wife mentioned this unusual phenomenon to Tesshu, he joked, "I guess my zazen is only good for rat poison." In fact, Tesshu discovered that if he glanced at the ceiling during zazen, mice would fall dead to the floor.

(Demon Zen really can be deadly. One of Zen Master Sozan's parishioners left his ancestral Nichiren temple because the priest there was so corrupt. Soon after joining Sozan's temple, the parishioner's wife died. Informed that a ghost was hanging around his wife's grave moaning, "I want to be buried in my family's Nichiren temple," the parishioner went to investigate and a ghost did indeed appear. Sozan accompanied the alarmed parishioner to the cemetery the following night. As soon as the ghost came forth, Sozan unleashed an earth-shattering KATSU!!! and the ghost fell out of sight. Following Sozan's instructions, the parishioner returned to the site in the morning and found the "ghost"—the evil Nichiren priest dressed in a white cloth—lying dead beside his wife's tombstone.)

During the first half of his tenure at the Imperial Household, Tesshu studied Zen under Seijo, abbot of Ryutakuji in Izu. After dinner on the eve of his monthly holiday, Tesshu would pack a few rice balls, tie on his straw sandals, and then head for Ryutakuji, a good seventy-five miles from Tokyo. Tesshu would arrive there by morning, consult with Seijo, have a light meal, and return home—a one-hundred-fifty-mile round trip made in a little more than one day. Some accounts state that Tesshu rode a horse part of the distance, but his closest disciples insisted that was a rare exception. Tesshu was never a good horseman and, at any rate, did not have the money to hire a horse. (Horses and horse-drawn carriages were

Mt. Fuji, inscribed with Tesshu's most famous waka poem, translated below.

a luxury in those days. Even when high officials such as Tesshu had free use of government-owned carriages, Tesshu preferred to walk. When asked why, Tesshu brushed a cartoon of a demon pulling a well-dressed gentleman in a carriage and added this inscription: "You may like to ride in a carriage, but I prefer this fire chariot because a demon never runs out of steam!")

Furthermore, Tesshu was incredibly fleet of foot. While on his mission to negotiate with Saigo during the civil war, a group of partisans dispatched an assassin to prevent Tesshu from reaching his destination. Tesshu moved at such a brisk pace that the assassin, even though he was running while Tesshu was walking, failed to catch up. The trip to Ryutakuji included long stretches of lonely mountain trails, and, on occasion, highwaymen would demand a "toll" from Tesshu before allowing him to pass. "You'll have to catch me to collect," Tesshu chuckled as he sped away.

After three years of instructing Tesshu, Seijo pronounced, "Your study here is finished." The puzzled Tesshu did not know what to make of this declaration because he still had many unresolved questions. As he pondered this enigma on his way back to Tokyo, Mt. Fuji suddenly came into view. "Oh!" Tesshu realized.

Perfect when clear,	*Harete yoshi*
Perfect when cloudy,	*kumoritemo yoshi*
Mt. Fuji's	*fuji no yama*
Original form	*moto no sugata wa*
Never changes.	*kawarazari keri*

When Tesshu ran back to Ryutakuji to thank Seijo for his teaching, he found the abbot waiting for him.

The last barrier Demon Tetsu had to pass was the "flashing swords" koan given him by Tekisui, abbot of Tenryuji in Kyoto. Whenever they met it was a clash of titans—each felt as if his life was on the line. During their *sanzen* (personal interview) encounters at Tesshu's home, the building shook with the sounds of Tekisui's tools—shouts, iron fists, a heavy stick—fashioning a new Tesshu.

Tekisui was exactly the no-nonsense, hardheaded type of Zen master Tesshu required. As a novice monk, he was so severely reprimanded by his teacher for spilling a bit of water, he took the name Tekisui, "drop of water." Lieutenant General Torio, a haughty Zen dilettante, enjoyed challenging Zen masters with his original koans. One day he invited Tekisui to his home for a meal and, after exchanging the customary pleasantries, asked if he could present one of his koans. "Sure," Tekisui consented, sensing an opportunity to tweak his pompous host's nose. Just as Torio opened his mouth to speak, Tekisui shoved him down. When the nonplussed general tried to rise, Tekisui knocked him down again. The third time, Tekisui pushed Torio so hard he flew out of the room into the garden. The servants working there shouted, "You've killed our master" and began pummeling Tekisui with their fists. Once order was restored, Tekisui warned Torio: "Beginners have no business composing their own koans."

Incidentally, Tekisui was an accomplished martial artist even though he never held a sword in his hands. Tesshu's disciple Murakami resented Takisui's rude treatment of his master—after all, Tesshu was an important government official who advised the Emperor himself. Murakami secretly vowed to dispose of the cheeky monk and one night tailed Tekisui, intent on cutting him in two. To Murakami's chagrin, whenever he was about to make a move, Tekisui would suddenly glance over his shoulder, turn a corner, or disappear in one of the temples along the way. Murakami tried again the next two nights but could get nowhere near the ever-elert Zen master. Murakami gave up and confessed his plot to Tesshu. Tesshu laughed: "You fool! Even if you had a score of accomplices, you would not be able to get near that master." Mortified, Murakami too began studying with Tekisui.

It is said that while Tesshu was struggling with this koan, he received a helpful clue to the riddle from a rich merchant. The merchant had come to Tesshu's home to request some calligraphy. During the course of their conversation, the merchant described the key to his success: "I was born into extreme poverty. With great difficulty, I amassed a small amount of capital and purchased some goods. The other merchants sensed that I was eager to sell my merchandise as quickly as possible and beat down my price. Later I stiffened my resolve and refused their low offers. My competitors raised the offers higher and higher but then I became greedy and wanted even more. Ultimately, I lost most of my capital. I did, however, learn a valuable lesson about the spirit of selling. Merchants should never be timid or concerned with victory or defeat, profit or loss. If one only thinks about making money, his heart pounds with anticipation; if he fears taking a beating, he will shrink and cower. Nothing can be accomplished by worrying about such things. It is best to keep one's heart clear, face the work at hand directly, and act boldly. I never cling to ideas of profit and loss—that is the key to my success as a businessman." Tesshu thus realized that the Way of a samurai and the Way of a merchant are not two different paths.

While Zen may make some people millionaires, it keeps others, such as Ragged Tetsu, penniless. Since Tesshu had distributed his inheritance among his siblings, he and his wife lacked money to set up house. They were so poor, in fact, that they had to sell off the few possessions they owned: the furniture, the cooking utensils, the sleeping quilts, and the *tatami* (straw mats). Only three tatami were left in the entire house: one for guests, one for themselves, and one, worn to shreds, for Tesshu's zazen. They averaged seven foodless days a month; Tesshu ate every other day for several extended periods. Because they had no sleeping quilts, Fusako gave birth to their first child on Tesshu's kimono while he attended her in his birthday suit. The child later died of malnutrition.

In Japan, it is the custom for all debts to be settled prior to the start of a new year. After downing a gift bottle of sake brought by a friend, a happily inebriated Tesshu recited this poem to the debt collectors gathered at his door:

> When you drink sake,
> You feel spring
> In your heart.
> Don't you debt collectors
> Hear the nightingale's song?

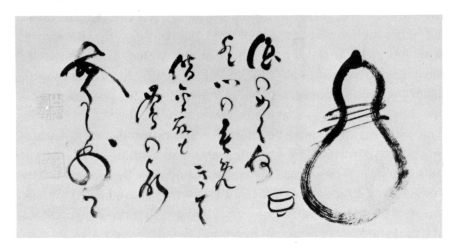

Sake gourd inscribed with the verse translated above.

They didn't. When they demanded their money, Tesshu came up with another verse:

> "Pay up!" you say,
> But I have no money.
> I sincerely want to
> Settle my debts—
> Please take that into this new year's account.

Tesshu opened his so-called "money" belt and pulled out two small pearls and a few coins: "Surely you don't want to deprive a samurai of his war funds." (Samurai were expected to always have enough money on their person to cover burial expenses.) Seeing no chance of getting their money, the merchants gave up and left.

Such extreme poverty was not at all uncommon during the chaotic last days of the Tokugawa Shogunate. Unlike most of his contemporaries who prospered after the Meiji Restoration, Tesshu remained broke despite his high salary from the Imperial Household.

In addition to his large immediate family of a wife and five children, Tesshu supported a small army of relatives, disciples, down-and-out friends, and assorted beggars—no deserving person was turned away from Tesshu's door. One building on his ramshackle estate was set aside for this group. Tesshu owed a fortune to money-lenders (much of it borrowed to prop up business ventures of his ne'er-do-well brother-in-law). The emperor kept giving him money for a new suit of clothes; invariably, it was passed on to one more needy. Half of Tesshu's dinner was left untouched so the maids, abandoned country girls Tesshu had taken in, could have extra food. When they protested, he told them he preferred the taste of daikon leaves, a "food" most people threw in the trash.

Tesshu's charity extended to other sentient beings as well. Upon learning that stray dogs in Tokyo were being clubbed to death when captured, Tesshu began hanging name tags around the neck of every homeless dog he came across. When the hapless animals were pursued by dogcatchers, they headed instinctively for the safety of Tesshu's property. Tesshu's pack of pet strays eventually grew so large that they consumed a bushel of rice every day. (Fortunately for Tesshu's many creditors, several of Tesshu's friends and former disciples were very wealthy men, and they settled Tesshu's debts following his death.)

As one of Japan's all-time great imbibers, Tesshu celebrated his great enlightenment in an appropriate manner. When Tekisui first met Tesshu after his disciple's breakthrough, he immediately sensed the trememdous change in Tesshu's bearing. No further testing was necessary—Tesshu had obviously arrived. Tekisui called for a case of beer to celebrate. Tesshu quaffed twelve bottles and exclaimed,

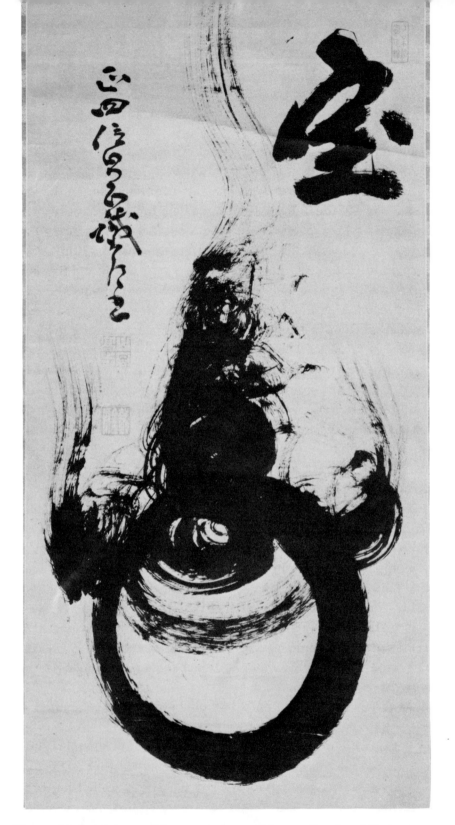

The *nyoi-hoju* (cintamani) is a marvelous wish-granting jewel that sprang from the brain of a dragon king. It can produce anything one desires in unlimited quantities. More than simply a symbol of good fortune, the nyoi-hoju stands for the inexhaustible riches of the Buddhist teaching. That is, as the single character inscription indicates, the real "treasure."

"I've never tasted anything so delicious!" He put away six more bottles with gusto before Tekisui admonished him gently, "You had better ease up. You've got a weak stomach you know."

"I guess I overdid it," roared Tesshu in the highest of spirits. Later, Tekisui presented Tesshu with an *inka*, a formal certificate of Dharma transmission.

Whenever Tesshu and a Zen master got together, sake, known among Buddhists as *hannya-to* ("hot water of transcendental wisdom"), flowed like water. Thanks to the generosity of his many friends and frequent gifts from the emperor, Tesshu was able to indulge in a half-gallon of transcendental wisdom every evening.

> In retirement from the world
> One learns the true meaning of wealth;
> In joyous intoxication
> One probes the ancient worlds.

Upon his great awakening in 1880, the externals of Tesshu's life remained the same; it was the inner transformation that enabled him to be teacher of the emperor, champion of Buddhism, and enlightened Zen master of priest and layman alike.

At the urging of Saigo Takamori, Katsu Kaishu, Iwakura Tomomi, and other important ministers who thought he would exert a steadying influence on Meiji, the impetuous young emperor, Tesshu agreed to serve in the Imperial Household for a ten-year period. Tesshu taught the emperor several significant lessons.

Meiji, a heavyset, powerful, vigorous man in his twenties, enjoyed sumo wrestling. He often wrestled with his aides, who, not surprisingly, let him win. This gave the emperor an inflated opinion of his ability and, furthermore, made him reckless—some of the aides were actually injured by his unbridled charges. Meiji also felt sure he could drink anyone under the table. One evening, as he and Tesshu were pouring down sake with the other aides, the discussion turned toward Japan's future as a country of civil law rather

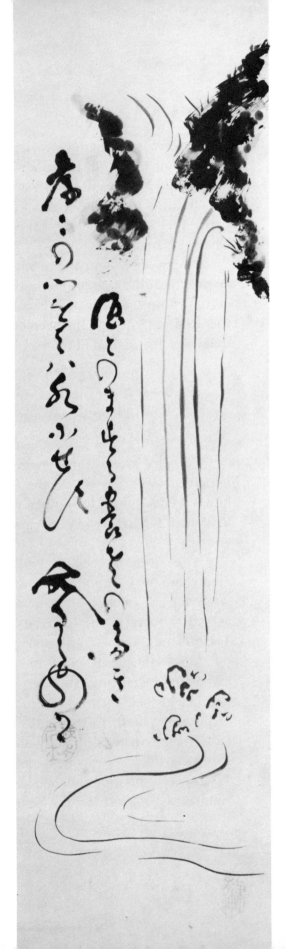

Waterfall.

Be filial to your aged relatives:
Instead of water
Provide them with a
gentle waterfall of sake
To ease their ills.

than imperial decree. When the emperor asked for Tesshu's opinion, he replied bluntly, "Well, if it is no longer an order, people will stop worshiping at the Imperial Shrine." This infuriated the emperor so much he challenged Tesshu to a sumo match.

When Tesshu politely refused, the enraged emperor tried to force Tesshu to stand. Meiji started shoving Tesshu but found him rooted to the ground like a giant tree. The emperor suddenly threw a punch at Tesshu's face; in a flash, Tesshu slightly shifted his position and the emperor flew past him crashing to the floor. Tesshu pinned Meiji there as the other aides screamed, "Stop it, Yamaoka! You're being disrespectful!"

"I know," glared Tesshu.

Tesshu went calmly into the next room waiting for the emperor to recover. The other aides demanded that he apologize immediately, but Tesshu refused. "If I let him throw me on purpose I would be nothing more than a lackey. I have pledged my life to his service, and would never do anything to hurt him. However, he must learn not to lose his temper when he drinks and not to bully others. If he does not learn how it feels to be thrown, he will become an impossible tyrant. When he comes to, tell him what I just said; if he orders me to commit seppuku, I will do so on the spot." After the emperor's senses returned, he sent a messenger to inform Tesshu that he was henceforth giving up both drinking and sumo. (A month later, Tesshu sent Meiji a case of wine, thus lifting the ban on alcohol.) Despite Tesshu's total candor, or perhaps because of it, Meiji trusted no one more.

Be it emperor or bureaucrat, Tesshu took no nonsense from anyone in the government. Against the total opposition of the entire palace staff and the government ministries, Tesshu insisted that the dying wish of a princess to have a Buddhist funeral rather than a State Shinto ceremony be honored. It was.

During a conference, the Minister of Education, an exceedingly obnoxious man named Mori, annoyed at Tesshu's habit of silently taking in all options being discussed, said in a mocking voice, "What is the matter with you? Are you a doll?" Tesshu turned his head slowly and then suddenly thrust his fan underneath Mori's chin, knocking the minister back in his seat. Towering over the smart aleck, Tesshu replied with a glare, "Yes, I'm a doll." (Mori, by the way, was later murdered by one of the people he insulted.)

One night, a group of disgruntled army officers attacked a command post near Take Bridge. Although the riot was not directed toward the emperor, the fighting spread near the vicinity of the palace. At the sound of gunfire, Tesshu sprang out of bed, pulled his *hakama* skirt over his nightshirt, grabbed his sword, and ran toward the palace. Without pausing to learn the nature of the disturbance, Tesshu headed straight for the emperor's room. Tesshu smashed down the heavy wooden storm doors and found Meiji standing alone—in their confusion, the palace guards had failed to assign someone to protect the emperor.

"Am I glad to see you!" the relieved emperor exclaimed. With his sword drawn, Tesshu stood guard by the emperor until the riot was put down and the all-clear given. Long after the peak of the fighting, the other aides began arriving, neatly dressed in their official attire. Tesshu begged the emperor's pardon for his highly unorthodox apparel, adding, "I did not think I had time to change." The emperor laughed heartily and asked Tesshu to leave his sword behind. "It will be a constant remainder of your courage and loyalty."

When Tesshu was on night duty, he slept in *seiza*, the formal samurai sitting position, for thirty minutes between his hourly rounds. The regular watchmen asked him, "Don't you get bored on night duty? Aren't you bothered by the striking of all these clocks?" (The emperor was very fond of clocks and the palace was full of them.)

"What does 'bored' mean?" Tesshu shot back. "The chiming of the clocks does not bother me at all—we sleep and wake in unison."

When an imperial tour to the Tohoku district was proposed, certain aides advised against it because that area was the last to capitulate to the new regime and there were still some pockets of resistance. Furthermore, they argued, what if a crisis occurs in Tokyo when the emperor is so far away? The emperor replied, "As long as Yamaoka is in charge here, there is no need for concern."

The emperor dispatched Tesshu to Kyushu to negotiate with recalcitrant Saigo Takamori, figuring that Tesshu was the only one in the government who commanded Saigo's respect. (Saigo once said

Formal portrait of Tesshu done in 1886 when he was fifty-one years old. The inscription reads:

> How many times was
>   my life in danger?
> Now I enjoy a
>   continuous banquet.
> Fifty-one years—
> A dusty head and
>   a dirty face.

The last line refers to the question: "What does a bodhisattva look like?" One must be not afraid to get into the thick of things, to mix it up with all types of people.

of Tesshu, "He doesn't need fame, fortune, status, or even life it-self—how do you deal with such man?") Although Tesshu did his best to dissuade Saigo from leaving the government, he sensed that Saigo must go his own way, however tragic. (Saigo rebelled, even-tually committing seppuku when his army was defeated by the Im-perial Forces, troops he once led.)

Although Tesshu accepted titles he received directly from the emperor, he severely criticized the custom of senior government of-ficials passing out honorary awards among themselves. When a member of one of those selection committees called on Tesshu to present him with an award, he let it be known exactly where they should put their medals. Upon notification of being named a "vis-count" in 1887, the year before his death, Tesshu composed this im-promptu verse:

> Just eating and sleeping
> Without doing a shred of work
> I've received this privilege:
> I may now be in the House of Lords
> But I'm still coughing blood.

(In the original, Tesshu substituted the homonym *kasoku*, "tribe of mosquitoes," for *kasoku*, "House of Lords.")

Both the emperor and empress were greatly saddened by Tes-shu's departure from the Imperial Household, but once his self-imposed term of ten years was up, he retired from government ser-vice to devote himself fully to his three Ways.

After a thousand years of imperial and military patronage, Bud-dhism was in jeopardy in Japan during the Meiji era. Now that the feudal system had been abolished, there would be no more lords to construct large "temple towns" near their castles (which could double as barracks) and to build magnificent cathedrals in memory of their ancestors (strategically located in case of a last-ditch defense). The government, intent on promoting indigenous State Shinto over imported Buddhism, decreed strict separation of shrine and temple. Not only was Buddhism losing its financial base, its teachings were also under attack. Many influential ministers and educators, believing that the superstitious doctrines of Buddhism impeded the modernization of the country, advocated abandonment of the religion altogether. Although outright suppression of Buddhism was rare, the "Abandon Buddhism, Eradicate Shakyamuni's Teaching" (*haibutsu-kishaku*) movement had numerous supporters and some deliberate destruction of temples and sutras did occur.

Tesshu appreciated the achievements of Western civilization, but he was also a firm defender of the glories of Oriental culture. He often declared, "I will continue to practice Buddhism even if I am the only one in the country to do so." Tesshu worked tirelessly to preserve "that which should be preserved" i.e., the teachings and practices which possess universal validity.

While serving as a government official in Shizuoka, Tesshu developed a keen interest in the life and teaching of Hakuin, the eighteenth century Rinzai Zen master. Tesshu admired Hakuin's zeal for practice, his pithy essays, his masterful brushwork, and, above all, his care and concern for ordinary folk. Because Hakuin spurned abbotship of a major temple, preferring to remain in his remote home district, he was not well known in the centers of power and had consequently never been awarded with the title of "National Teacher," an honor routinely bestowed on outstanding priests. In order to rectify this serious oversight and to bring Hakuin's teaching the wide recognition it deserved, Tesshu organized a committee to promote Hakuin's designation as a "National Teacher." Their efforts bore fruit, and in 1885 Emperor Meiji declared Hakuin *Shoshu Kokushi*, "National Teacher of the Right Tradition." Tesshu also helped restore Shoju-an in Tokyo, the former hermitage of Hakuin's teacher, Shoju Etan.

Tesshu was instrumental in the restoration of several large temples formerly under imperial patronage. While accompanying the emperor on a tour of western Japan, Tesshu learned that Kokutaiji

The inscription on Tesshu's painting of Buddha's birth reproduces Shakyamuni's bold declaration, "In heaven and earth I alone am the only Honored One." In a sense, this shout of life is repeated each time a newborn utters its first cry. It is an announcement of one's original and absolute nature, empty and clear with no trace of duality or duplicity. It also suggests the truth that each sentient being is an "only Honored One." Thus, it is futile to clutch at outside things; each and every individual is a complete universe.

It is often said that a painting of Bodhidharma, the Grand Patriarch of Zen Buddhism, is really a spiritual self-portrait—one must become a Bodhidharma in order to brush a good one. Consciously or not, Tesshu has painted himself here. The inscription, "Vast emptiness, nothing holy," was Bodhidharma's reply to Emperor Wu's question, "What is the first principle of Buddhism?"

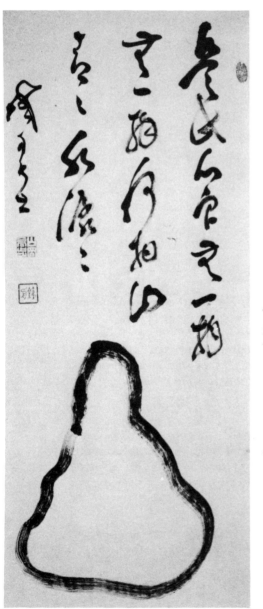

This single stroke Bodhidharma is inscribed with one of Tesshu's favorite verses:

> This is the Mind-seal of not
>   one thing.
> What is "not one thing?"
> Mountains fresh and green,
> Water clear and flowing.

Tesshu once composed this humorous *senryu*:

> Perfect plum blossoms:
> My purse too contains
> Not one thing.

Left, The Heart of Sutra Mantra:
Gone, gone, gone beyond,
gone completely beyond,
Enlightenment, hail!" (*Gyatei,
gyatei, hara gyatei, haraso gyatei,
boji sowaka*).

Right, Hail to the Lotus Sutra of
the Marvelous Law: (*Namu myoho
renge kyo*).

Left, Demon-rod by Hakuin, Tesshu's favorite Zen master, and *right*, Tesshu's version. The inscriptions on both say: Whoever fears this demon-rod will be on the way to paradise.

in Toyama Prefecture had fallen into ruin. Since Tesshu had no money to donate, he used his brush to raise funds. Tesshu wrote 10,000 large sheets of calligraphy—primarily the Zen poems of Kanzan (Han-shan), the eighth century Chinese eccentric—that were mounted on 1,200 folding screens. The screens were sold, proceeds going to the Kokutaiji reconstruction fund.

Upon completion of all 1,200 screens, a special thanksgiving banquet was held at a large Tokyo temple. Two thousand wandering musicians, vagabond craftsmen, and just plain derelicts were rounded up and invited to attend the feast, where they were served the finest vegetarian fare and treated to an unlimited amount of sake. At the end of the banquet, Tesshu and the other officials bowed deeply to the guests, handing each one a "thank you" envelope containing a small gift of money. Carriages were waiting to return the guests to their "residences."

"Where to, sir?"

"Who me? Oh, yes. Take me to Ocha no Mizu . . . underneath the bridge there."

"Pure wind, bright moon" (*Seifu meigetsu*) brushed by Tesshu on the sliding doors in the Buddha Hall of Yokoji in Ishikawa Prefecture.

Tesshu helped restore two other major temples: he donated 6,500 pieces of calligraphy to Yokoji, a lovely old Soto Zen temple in Ishikawa Prefecture, and supported the reconstruction of Shizuoka's Kunoji, renamed Tesshuji in honor of its main patron.

Zensho-an, the temple Tesshu founded in memory of all those slain in the turmoil of the civil war, had an interesting genesis. Every day on his way to the palace, Tesshu would admire a signboard hanging above a nearby rice-cake shop. The three large characters *Zen-Sho-An* were brushed by Rankei Doryu, the Chinese priest who brought Rinzai Zen to Japan in the thirteenth century. Tesshu learned from the owner of the store that Rankei had resided briefly in that area, upon his arrival from China, living in a small hermitage he named Zensho-an. When Rankei departed for Kamakura to instruct the Hojo Shogun, he presented the signboard to his host, the present owner's ancestor. Because Tesshu liked the calligraphy so much, the shopowner gave it to him. "*Zensho*" means "live completely" with every ounce of one's strength in the present moment; it also means "die completely" without hesitation or regret—a perfect name for Tesshu's own temple (*an*). Esso, the priest Tesshu invited to be the first abbot of the temple, was the ideal choice. Like Tesshu, Esso was dying of stomach cancer and every minute of life was "zensho." Zensho-an has lived up to its name: it has burned down twice in its brief history, each occasion rising from the ashes in renewed splendor.

The Great Sumida River Memorial Service, one of the largest religious gatherings of the Meiji era, was sponsored by Tesshu. Originally intended as a memorial service for victims of the Tempo famines, it grew to include all those who had perished without a proper burial in the previous fifty years. Over a thousand priests assembled to chant sutras for the occasion and a huge crowd of mourners lined the sides of the river to float stupa boats, bearing the names of the deceased, across the water.

Just as Tesshu was not a popularizer of kendo, neither was he a popularizer of Buddhism. When a priest complimented Tesshu on his successful efforts to promote Zen, he responded sharply, "There may be more Zen temples with more parishioners these days, but that does not mean Zen is flourishing. In fact, whenever Zen attempts to win converts or compete with other sects its true spirit is lost. Nothing I have done was for the sake of popularizing Zen; I've simply worked to strengthen and deepen the practice of Zen which I consider the heart of Buddhism. If just one person carries on the right transmission, I will be satisfied."

Tesshu was always a popular figure. Following his enlightenment, there came an unbroken stream of visitors to his home. As before, callers included those who merely wanted to borrow money or to have some petition presented to the emperor, but most came for instruction and counsel, and not a few hung around just to absorb a bit of the tremendous energy radiated by Tesshu's presence. There were students, for instance, who did zazen in the crumbling entrance hall of Tesshu's house—the only space available—because that alone gave them inspiration. Despite the constant crush of visitors, Tesshu's door was always open and all were received with courtesy.

Chiba Rozo, Tesshu's physician, played Dr. Watson to Tesshu's Sherlock Holmes. Chiba, the Yamaoka family doctor for years, hardly said a word outside of examinations. One day after a house call, Tesshu invited him to stay for tea.

"I've heard that you are a good doctor, but I'm afraid I don't have much confidence in you," Tesshu confessed. "Do you know the saying, 'No rider above the saddle, no horse beneath it?' That is the secret of any art—becoming one with technique. You seem too distant from your patients—I fear you cannot understand what ails them and thus cure their illnesses."

"You may be an expert swordsman and a high government official, but it is obvious you know nothing about medicine," retorted Chiba as he got up to leave.

Actually, Chiba was stung by Tesshu's accusation and, on his next visit, asked, "What method do you suggest I follow?"

"You are too impatient so it would be a waste of time to tell you."

"I'm as patient as the next man," yelled Chiba impatiently.

"Well, then," Tesshu told him, "ponder this verse for a while: 'In the cosmos, not a single day; only one person in heaven and earth.' When you've got the meaning, let me know."

With great difficulty Chiba finally penetrated this first barrier. Tesshu handed him a new problem: "Right now where is the spirit of a superior man?" Chiba eventually solved this and other koans Tesshu served up, becoming a confirmed Zen practitioner. To inspire him, Tesshu presented Chiba with a calligraphy by Hakuin Zenji. It read: "SETTLED—fix yourself in the best place; know exactly where to stop."

Unfortunately, Chiba got it in his head that one had to be a monk in order to engage in real Zen practice. Tesshu told him that such a move was premature; Chiba had much work to do in the world. Since Chiba was adamant, Tesshu wrote him a letter of introduction to Tekisui.

"What will you do as a monk?" Tekisui inquired of Chiba. The doctor had not thought about that. "Solve the koan 'Arrive at the Way with no difficulty' and I'll accept you as my disciple." Try as he might, Chiba could not pass this gateless gate, and abandoned his plans to renounce the world, much to Tesshu's and Tekisui's great relief.

One day Chiba declared: "To really practice zazen, it is necessary to cut off sexual passion."

"That's quite an exalted state you are aiming for," laughed Tesshu. "Sexual passion is the root of all existence. How do you propose to cut it off?"

"By separating myself from my wife and all other women; then sexual temptation will not arise."

"That's rather selfish, isn't it? What will happen to your wife, a faithful companion for twenty years? That is no way to cut off sexual passion—that is merely suppressing it."

"Then what should I do to eradicate sexual passion?"

"Throw yourself into the world of sexual passion, exhaust all its possibilities, and then you will find release. Love your wife with all your heart and attain enlightenment in the midst of everyday life."

While they were discussing this sensitive problem, Bokuju, abbot of Kyoto's Daitokuji, happened to stop by. Asked for his opinion on the matter, he mumbled something about "the old woman burning the hermitage" and beat a hasty retreat.*

Tesshu continued, "In my twenties and early thirties I was obsessed with the dimensions of sexual passion. I slept with thousands of women, hoping to bridge the gap between man and woman, self and other. Even after my great realization at age forty-five, the problem persisted. Not until my forty-ninth year, following another profound enlightenment experience, was I finally able to transcend sexual passion."

A friend who was also present suggested that Tesshu was just getting old. "No," Tesshu shook his head. "What you mean by sexual passion is 'physical lust.' That ceased to trouble me in my mid-thirties. If one cannot penetrate sexual passion—the root of samsara and the basic life-force of the material world—to its source, one's enlightenment is incomplete."

Understandably, Tesshu's wife was not sympathetic to his earlier "practice of sexual passion" however necessary he felt it to be for his spiritual development. Pressed by her family to divorce him, and unable to bear his daily practice sessions with other women, Fusako confronted Tesshu. Although Tesshu did his best to explain the true nature of his practice, she was not convinced. Brandishing a dagger, Fusako swore she would kill herself and the children if he did not stop running around. He stopped.

---

*An old woman built a hermitage for a monk and supported him for twenty years. One day to test the level of his enlightenment she sent a young girl to seduce him. When the girl embraced the monk, he recited this verse: "A withered tree among the frozen rocks; not a trace of warmth for three winters." Upon learning of the monk's response, the old woman chased him out and put the hermitage to the torch.

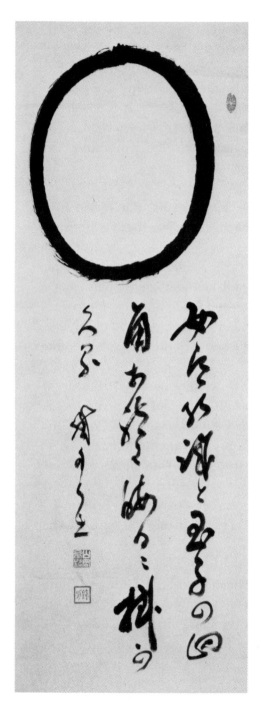

Although "not one thing" would be an appropriate accompanying verse for this Zen circle (*enso*), Tesshu selected one more down to earth:

> If there are sincere courtesans and square eggs,
> Hang this up on the last day of the month.

(An old song from the Yoshiwara pleasure quarters runs:

> If there are sincere courtesans and square eggs,
> A full moon will appear on the last day of the month.

During his practice of sexual passion, Tesshu spent a lot of time in the pleasure quarters, frequently "on the house"—the girls did not demand payment from their demon lover. Rumor has it that one of the young geishas went so far as to refuse being "ransomed" by a rich patron in order to continue meeting Tesshu. Tesshu had to persuade her to take the precious opportunity.) Courtesans are not sincere, eggs are not square—these are facts of life. In a similar vein, Tesshu wrote on a painting of a fan:

> As soon as the flies retreat,
> The mosquitoes advance.
> Don't miss the June bargain sales!

No amount of enlightenment can alter the way things are; it is our perceptions, not the world itself, that must be transformed.

Tesshu's ideas about practice were unorthodox, to say the least. Once one of his live-in disciples, unaccustomed to the luxury of meat and alcohol, vomited during the memorial party held March 31, the anniversary of Tesshu's enlightenment. Tesshu scooped up the vomit and swallowed it.

"Sensei! What are you doing?" his amazed disciples cried.

"I'm practicing 'no distinction between the pure and the impure.'"

"But that is poison you are eating!"

"If you worry about your body, you will be afraid to tackle anything. On the other hand, if your practice is solid, there is nothing you cannot handle."

There is another, equally unpalatable, version of this story. One of the beggars attending the Kokutaiji banquet mentioned above vomited. Tesshu scooped it up and invited the roshis present to partake of this special Buddha food. When they declined the offer, Tesshu said in a surprised tone, "I didn't know Buddhist priests could be so picky. I'll have to eat it myself!"

It may well be that both versions actually occurred. Buddhist priests of all sects enjoyed being with Tesshu, but they were occasionally in for a hard time. Tesshu had a high regard for Unsho Ritsushi, a Shingon priest who strictly observed the full monastic discipline. Tesshu's wife and children studied with this priest. When Unsho was ready to give lay ordination to Tesshu's family, he asked Tesshu if he too would like to receive the Bodhisattva precepts.

"How can I receive something that has no form?" Tesshu asked.

No reply.

One morning Unsho visited Tesshu to discuss an important matter pertaining to Mt. Koya, the headquarters of Shingon Buddhism in Japan. Tesshu, human after all, was under the weather and Unsho was informed that he was not receiving visitors that day. Unsho, evidently unable to believe that Tesshu was actually ill, came back later that afternoon.

Tesshu came out in his nightshirt and asked Unsho: "Is there a precept requiring monks to harass sick people?"

Again, no reply.

Abbots who drank too much or otherwise behaved badly were corralled in temples that Tesshu had restored; there he could keep an eye on them. With the sole exception of Tekisui, there was not a single Buddhist priest in the country who could hold his own with Tesshu.

Zen cartoon of Tesshu's colorful contemporary, the Zen priest Nantembo. Nantembo was famous for his uninhibited use of his nanten staff to discipline his disciples. The inscription to the left is by Takahashi Deishu:

> Can you wake up?
> Or not?
> Regardless,
> You get a taste of
>   my staff
> Sorry about that!

(Incidentally, Nantembo was one of the roshis Tesshu kept on a short leash—when intoxicated, Nantembo used his staff too indiscriminately.)

Tesshu never recommended zazen to his friends or forced his disciples to sit. If, however, one asked to practice, look out!

Sanyutei Encho, a professional storyteller of some renown, called on Tesshu one day. Tesshu said, "I hear that you are a famous storyteller. Please tell me one."

"Any favorites?"

"How about Momotaro?"

Sanyutei, slightly offended by Tesshu's request for the most common of all Japanese folktales, rattled off the story.

"That was awful," Tesshu complained. "My mother's version was far better. Your Momotaro never came alive—you used your mouth too much."

Sanyutei thought to himself, "How can a storyteller tell a story without using his mouth?"

Some days later, Sanyutei mentioned to Tesshu that he was interested in giving zazen a try. "When would be a convenient time to begin?"

"Right now."

"But. . . ."

"Why wait to try a good thing?" said Tesshu as he led Sanyutei to a spare room on the second floor. After setting up a screen around Sanyutei and showing him how to sit, Tesshu told him, "You can get up to go to the toilet and take a short break when your meals are brought; otherwise, you must sit here and ponder MU (nothingness)."

When Sanyutei failed to return home that evening, his wife sent one of her husband's disciples to inquire after the missing storyteller. "He cannot leave here until he solves the problem I gave him," the disciple was told. Sanyutei's theater manager, desperate to gain release of his star attraction, was given the same answer. Sanyutei's escape attempt was thwarted by Tesshu's dreadful stare. Resigned to the situation, Sanyutei gave himself wholeheartedly to MU. A week later he had it.

"Tell me the story of Momotaro again," Tesshu demanded. Sanyutei did so. "Now that is really Momotaro. Tell every story like that

The mark of an enlightened master is a wide circle of acquaintances. Tesshu had contacts with most of the outstanding figures of the day. Basho's famous frog poem calligraphed by Tesshu on a painting by Shibata Zeshin, a noted Meiji era artist.

(detail) *Furu ike ya kawazu tobikomu mizu no oto*

The old pond:
a frog leaps in
the sound of water.

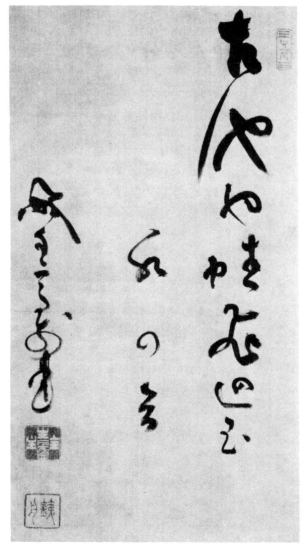

and you will be the finest master in Japan." Sanyutei later received the Buddhist name *Musetsu*, "No Tongue," from Tekisui.

A young man from the country wanted Tesshu to help him obtain a government job. "My family lost everything during the civil war and I hope to restore its once good fortune," he explained. Tesshu, an excellent judge of character, thought the earnest young man deserved a chance. "To become a government employee a certain amount of education is necessary. Have you done much studying?" Tesshu asked.

"Unfortunately, no. There was no money for schooling."

Tesshu thought for a minute and then said, "I want you to tell me what 'not one thing' means. Think it over day and night and do not come back here until you have an answer."

After much deliberation, the young man was able to present an acceptable reply. Tesshu gave him several more koans to solve. Satisfied with the young man's education, Tesshu recommended him for a position and the young man went on to become an exemplary civil servant.

A visitor said to Tesshu, "I suppose your wife and children are accomplished practitioners of zazen?"

"No. Since they lack the inclination they do not practice zazen. A Shingon priest is giving them instruction in Buddhist teachings."

"Surely there is no distinction in Zen between men and women, young and old, wise and foolish."

"Of course not. However, Zen requires a lot of stamina and a certain kind of perseverance. If not suited to one's physical and mental capabilities, zazen is useless."

One fellow wanted to take up Zen in order to free himself of the various afflictions that plague human beings; he wanted to "slide through life free of stress." Tesshu was blunt: "In my Zen, if you are a samurai, you walk the way of a samurai; if you are a merchant, you walk the way of a merchant. The kind of Zen you want is best taken up with a clown." In other words, one must face the problems of existence directly and not try to escape one's duties.

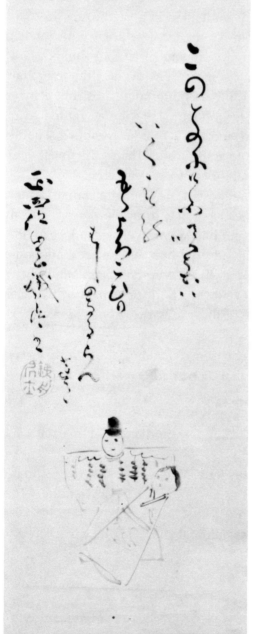

Painting of two *hinasama* dolls with Tesshu's calligraphy of a poem by his friend Rengetsu, the talented nun-poet-calligrapher-potter.

> Today, as an offering
> To this lord and lady
> One of early spring's
>   treasures—
> Freshly opened
> Peach blossoms.

Hinasama dolls are displayed on March third, Girl's Day.

A Buddhist layman was eager to hear Tesshu discourse on the *Sayings of Rinzai*. When Tesshu informed him that Kosen Roshi was lecturing on that text regularly in Kamakura, the layman said, "I know. I want to hear *your* discourse."

"Very well," Tesshu agreed and led the guest to the training hall. There he demonstrated swordsmanship with one of his disciples. "What do you think about my discourse on the *Sayings of Rinzai*?" When there was no reply, Tesshu explained, "Since I am a swordsman I best express my understanding of Rinzai's teaching through the Way of the Sword. No matter how great your intellectual comprehension, if you mimic someone else, your Zen is dead."

Hiranuma Senzo, said by some to be the wealthy merchant whose story spurred Tesshu on to enlightenment, lost his beloved daughter to a fatal disease. Despondent, Hiranuma wanted to renounce this vale of tears and become a monk. Tesshu dissuaded him: "Use your vast resources to assist others; that is the finest offering you could ever make in memory of your dead child."

In a similar case, Tesshu suggested the opposite course. Amata Guan, a noted waka poet, was separated from his parents during the confusion of the civil war and had spent twenty years searching for them all over Japan. Tesshu advised him to take ordination and organize memorial services for all those who had been similarly afflicted. Tesshu wrote letters of introduction for Amata to two Zen masters: "Become the disciple of the one with whom you feel most comfortable."

One day, a mountain ascetic from Takayama showed up at Tesshu's door. "You won't believe this! I've made myself invulnerable to fire."

"Sure you have," sighed Tesshu.

"No, it's true! Can you arrange an audience for me with the emperor?"

"Of course not." The ascetic refused to budge, however, and because he claimed to be an old acquaintance of Tesshu's father, Tesshu agreed to a demonstration.

A fire was made in the garden and the household gathered to

witness the "miracle." The ascetic changed into a white robe, concentrated intently for several minutes, and then plunged his right arm into the heart of the fire. In a few seconds, a terribly pained expression appeared on his face. As the ascetic teetered Tesshu ordered his disciples to save him. When the ascetic regained consciousness, he moaned, "It always worked before." His horribly burned arm had to be amputated (with Tesshu footing the bill). Under certain conditions, *yamabushi* apparently can make themselves impervious to fire; in this case, it is likely that the aura of Tesshu's conviction that "there is nothing mysterious in the Buddhist Law" inhibited the ascetic's mental power.

Another time, a fervent disciple of the famous Russian Orthodox missionary Nicolai tried to convert Tesshu to Christianity. Tesshu, weary of the young man's irrational persistence, came up with this koan: "If you discovered someone greater than Jesus, what would you do?"

"I'd gladly become his follower, but I don't believe that there is anyone greater than Jesus in this world."

"You are wrong. There is one greater right here," said Tesshu as he pointed to himself. The young proselytizer never bothered Tesshu again, and, in fact, later abandoned Christianity.

Tesshu had a zany Zen sense of humor. On the way home from an errand, Tesshu and a friend decided to take in part of a sumo tournament then being held in Tokyo. After watching a few of the matches, Tesshu suddenly removed his shoes and climbed up on the ring, still wearing his frock coat and top hat. "It's a foreigner!" the spectators roared with glee. "This should be interesting! Hang in there!" Dressed in such apparel, six-feet tall with a full beard, Tesshu did indeed have the appearance of a westerner.

When the embarrassed wrestlers did not respond to the challenge, Tesshu pointed to the largest one present and motioned him up to the ring. Tesshu secured a firm hold on the wrestler's sash and moved him back to the edge of the ring. Instead of shoving him out,

Tesshu released his grip, slapped the wrestler playfully on the back, and descended from the ring. "Wow!" the audience screamed. "That foreigner is really strong! More! More!" Waving to the delighted crowd, Tesshu left the arena in triumph.

Westernized Japanese adopted the custom of throwing elaborate "Charity Balls" to display both their philanthropy and their latest finery. To be considered a success, such balls needed top-rate entertainment. When Tesshu sponsored a charity ball of his own, the assembled guests eagerly awaited the splendid entertainment this important government official would surely arrange. The curtain opened and Tesshu presented the feature act—a large group of shabbily dressed blind fortune tellers and masseuses. On Tesshu's cue, the women performed their particular "hidden talents"—some played the shamisen, some blew flutes, some recited Shinto prayers, some sang popular songs—all at once in an incredible cacophony. "This, ladies and gentlemen," Tesshu announced playfully to the startled audience, "is an Oriental-style Charity Ball!"

Upon Tesshu's retirement from the Imperial Household, his daily schedule consisted of swordsmanship from 6:00 to 9:00 in the morning, calligraphy and painting from 10:00 to 4:00 or 5:00, and zazen or sutra-copying at night (often until 1:00 or 2:00 in the morning). Tesshu faithfully adhered to the Zen adage; "When hungry eat, when tired sleep"; whenever he felt sleepy Tesshu would excuse himself, retire to his room, nap soundly for a half-hour or so (snoring like a tiger), and then return to his work or guests totally refreshed.

The years of hard training and heavy drinking eventually took their toll and Tesshu's ailment was diagnosed as stomach cancer. Tesshu maintained his daily schedule to the very end, without complaint or resignation, concentrating on the matters at hand while letting pleasure and pain, life and death flow naturally.

His wife wondered if Tesshu had any golden words of wisdom for posterity.

"No."

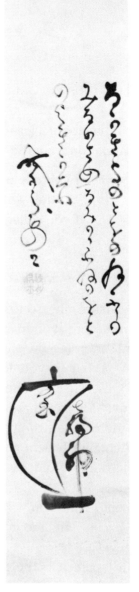

Zen bat.

> Aren't there any birds
> around here?
> This cheeky bat has let his
> whiskers grow
> And is lording it over everything.

This Zen bat has taken over the world, sporting in perfect freedom. Tesshu also brushed Zen slugs and Zen maggots. Although the paintings have apparently vanished, there is a record of their inscriptions:

(Zen slug)
> In this world
> Snakes and frogs
> Are terrifying
> But luckily there are
> A lot of slugs [for them to eat].

(For some reason, certain Japanese are as frightened by frogs and toads as they are of snakes.)

(Zen maggots)
> Maggots may thrive in shit
> But don't try to destroy them;
> Many beneficial things
> Come from shit,
> You know.

Treasure Boat of the Seven Gods of Good Fortune. Here Tesshu has playfully combined calligraphy, painting, and Zen humor. The nonsense verse, which reads the same backward or forward, says:

> After a long night
> All the gods awake
> From their slumber
> Stirred by the sound
> of waves
> Striking the boat.

"What about a legacy for your grandchildren?" Tesshu brushed this quotation from the Chinese sage, Ssu-ma:

> If you pile up money for your descendants,
>   they will be certain to waste it;
> If you collect books for them,
>   be certain that they won't read a word.
> It is better to accumulate hidden virtue,
>   for that will last a long time.

Matsuoka heard that Tesshu was sinking fast. He sneaked into Tesshu's room at night and jumped on his teacher who was sitting in zazen. After Tesshu pinned the intruder, he saw that it was Matsuoka. "What are you doing, you fool!"

"Oh, Sensei! There is nothing wrong with you! You are still healthy!" Matsuoka ran to Fusako to report the good news that her husband was as strong as ever.

Actually, Tesshu had only one more week of life. Hundreds of people came to bid Tesshu farewell including his older colleague, Kaishu.

"Looks like you will be leaving before I will," said Kaishu.

"Excuse me for going first," Tesshu joked. "I'm on urgent business."

In Japan, it is the custom to bring a seriously ill person gifts, often in the form of money. Tesshu left careful instructions that this money be distributed to those needy persons who had been recently turned away—Tesshu had completely run out of funds.

When it came time to die on July 19, 1888, Tesshu bathed and put on a spotless white kimono. Following convention, his disciples requested a death verse. Tesshu immediately chanted this haiku:

> Tightening my abdomen
>   against the pain—
> The caw of a morning crow.

(Since his disciples had never heard of a death verse with the word "pain" in it—they thought "peace," "light," or a similar sentiment

Tesshu's representation of the Fudo Myoo worshiped at the huge Shingon temple in Narita. Fudo (Acala), epitome of fiery dynamism and invincible imperturbability, is a patron saint of swordsmen. He is customarily accompanied by two boy attendants who assist him in his work of subduing evil and promoting awakening. The inscription consists of the brief *Holy Fudo Sutra:*

> Once during an assembly of Buddha's followers, Fudo appeared. This Fudo was tremendously powerful: great compassion was evident in his pale dark complexion, great stability was obvious as he assumed the Diamond Seat, and great wisdom was manifest in the flames surrounding him. Brandishing a sword of insight he cut through the three poisons of greed, anger, and delusion; his samadhi-rope bound the enemies of Buddhism. Formless like the empty space of the Dharma Body, Fudo settles nowhere but lives in the heart of sentient beings. Devoted servant of all, he encourages the well-being and ultimate salvation of sentient beings. When the entire assembly heard this teaching they joyously believed and received it.

This was painted only four months before Tesshu's death; no one could ever guess it to be the brushwork of a man terminally ill with stomach cancer.

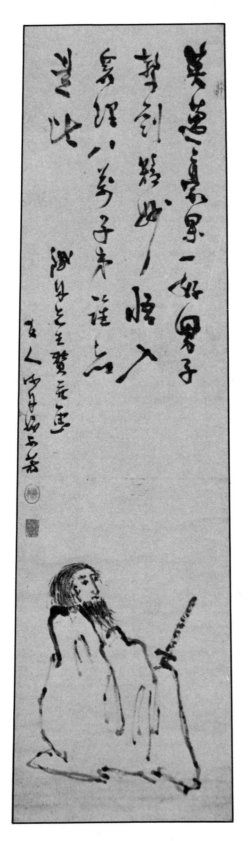

Zen sketch of Tesshu by Katsu Kaishu. The inscription says:

> Brave and wise, this
>   virile man accomplished
>   great things.
> His swordsmanship was
>   incomparably sublime,
> His enlightenment all-
>   embracing.
> Will future generations
>   ever produce an equal?

would be more appropriate for a Zen master—they were hesitant to make it public. With trepidation, they gave the verse to the Abbot Gasan when he asked for it. "What a magnificent death verse," he exclaimed. When the crow flew past and cried out, Tesshu was hemorrhaging, his stomach eaten away by his cancer—those two events filled the cosmos.)

Tesshu placed himself in formal zazen posture, bid his family and friends goodbye ("Don't worry about food or clothing," he cautioned his eldest son), closed his eyes, took a deep breath, and entered eternal meditation. Some accounts state that Tesshu seemed to smile serenely just before his death. He was fifty-three years old.

Five thousand people attended Tesshu's funeral, jointly officiated by the primates of all the major Buddhist sects. Fusako, his beloved companion, died ten years later to the day. Tesshu is buried at Zensho-an, once again united with his family and many of his closest disciples.

Tesshu's Zen was a constant flame of unfettered activity: bravery coupled with compassion, iron discipline combined with fluid response, physical vigor harmonized with spiritual refinement. Tekisui composed this memorial verse for Tesshu's funeral:

> Sword and brush poised between the Absolute
>   and the Relative,
> His loyal courage and noble strength pierced the Heavens.
> A dream of fifty-three years,
> Enveloped by the pure fragrance of a lotus
>   blooming in the midst of a roaring fire.

This tear-stained death portrait was done on the spot by Tanaka Seiji, one of Tesshu's disciples. July 19, 1888, was a sweltering summer day, hence the fan—even in death, Zen teaches us to be hot when it is hot and cold when it is cold. Although it is the ideal form of transition, very few Zen practitioners actually enter eternal meditation in the zazen posture; Tesshu is thought to be the only one in the Meiji era to have done so. Because such a death is so rare, his friends and disciples considered delaying Tesshu's cremation to let him "sit in state." However, since Tesshu never liked to be on display, they decided against it.

Every July 19th a special memorial service is held for Tesshu at Zensho-an. These three scrolls are hung above the altar. *Right:* Sitting in the midst of a thousand sages. *Left:* Shattering the fortress of a demon-army. The portrait of Tesshu bears Tekisui's memorial verse:

> Sword and brush poised between the Absolute
>   and the Relative,
> His loyal courage and noble strength pierced
>   the Heavens.
> A dream of fifty-three years,
> Enveloped by the pure fragrance of a lotus flower
>   blooming in the midst of a roaring fire.

Skulls have always been a popular theme of Zen art, not primarily as symbols of impermanence and the vanity of life, but as a representation of the rightness of change, the Buddha-nature inherent in the inevitable dissolution of all things. Tesshu's inscriptions bears this out:

> There is no greater matter of congratulation than this!

On another skull painting he wrote:

> Cut off death
> And you will have only bliss;
> Imitate a dead man
> And you will be worse off
> Than a corpse.

4

 THE ASCENDING DRAGON

Despite his unparalleled accomplishments, Tesshu was no natural genius. His memory was poor and the only way he could retain what he read was to copy it several times. While his innate ability was not great, Tesshu's effort was supreme—it is likely that Tesshu produced more pieces than any other calligrapher in Oriental history.

When Tesshu was living in Takayama, he had the good fortune to become the disciple of Iwasa Ittei, fifty-first Headmaster of the *Jubokudo* School of Calligraphy. The name *juboku*, "enter the wood," is derived from the following legend: once someone mistakenly tried to efface writing brushed on a board by the third century Chinese calligrapher-saint O Gishu (Wang Hsi-chih); regardless of how deeply he cut, it was impossible to erase the brush strokes—the characters themselves, not just the ink, had penetrated the heart of the wood. In the ninth century, the Jubokudo School was transmitted from China to Japan by the Shingon patriarch Kobo Daishi. The emphasis in Jubokudo calligraphy is on the spiritual, rather than the technical, aspects of brushwork.

Iwasa, disciple and successor of the Tendai priest Jokei, too was a demon for training. He spent three years practicing nothing but the single-stroke character *ichi* (one), and used a pint of ink a day during regular training. In order to be accepted as Iwasa's student, a candidate was required to submit a copy of the "One-Thousand-

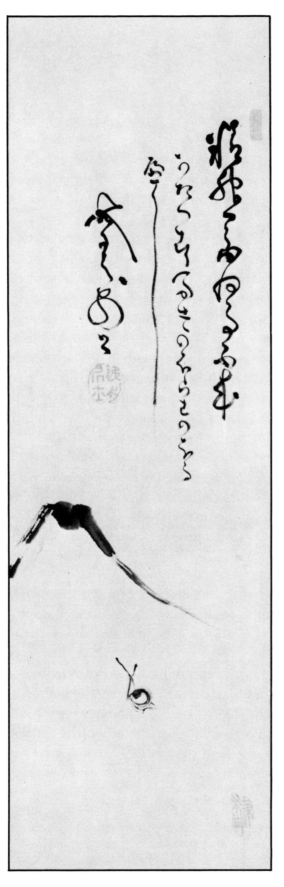

Left, Ascending dragon. One creature soars to the top of Mt. Fuji in a flash while (*right*) the other inches its way up to the peak over years and months— both the dragon and the snail reach the intended destination according to their respective pace. After writing the poem

> If this snail
> Sets out for
> The top of Fuji
> Surely he will
> Get there

Tesshu asked his disciples to add a suitable inscription. No one volunteered, so Tesshu brushed his favorite saying along the right side:

> Unified in spirit what
>   cannot be accomplished?

Character Classic" (*Senjimon*), the standard primer. After a month of studying Iwasa's model book, Tesshu was instructed by his father to make a clean copy of the text on formal paper. The eleven-year-old boy immediately set to work and in a few hours handed his father a sixty-three sheet copy. Amazed at the boy's aptitude, Iwasa agreed to teach Tesshu.

There is some question regarding Tesshu's status as fifty-second Headmaster of the Jubokudo School. At age fifteen, Tesshu submitted a formal "Request for Instruction"; a scant six months later he received a "Certificate of Mastery" from Iwasa. That, in itself, is not so unusual—obviously Tesshu was Iwasa's student prior to submitting that document—but it is improbable that Iwasa would designate as his successor a fifteen-year-old youth with only four years of training, no matter how talented. It is speculated that Iwasa, then seventy years old and without any other promising disciples, considered Tesshu able enough to carry on the Jubokudo tradition but was reluctant to declare him head of such an important school at that tender age. Teacher and disciple corresponded regularly until Iwasa's death in 1858. Thereafter, Tesshu studied on his own, visiting exhibitions, consulting with scholars, and, above all, copying classics of Chinese calligraphy. Because no other worthy claimant appeared, Tesshu naturally assumed the mantle of the fifty-second, and last, Headmaster of the Jubokudo School of Calligraphy.

The early samples of Tesshu's calligraphy, dating from his late thirties and early forties, are technically adequate but lack depth. Not until his enlightenment at age forty-five did his brushwork truly mature.

Tesshu's output the last eight years of his life was prodigious—conservatively estimated at a MILLION works of art. The main reason for such astounding productivity was to raise money for the restoration of temples, for disaster victims, and other worthy causes. In addition to the 12,000-sheet 1,200 screens for Kokutaiji and the 6,500 pieces for Yokoji, Tesshu wrote 20,000 sheets for another set of

Top, Tesshu's copy of the Senjimon made when he was eleven years old. *Middle,* Fifteen-year-old Tesshu's "Formal Petition" to become Iwasa Ittei's disciple. *Bottom,* Iwasa's calligraphy of *Ichirakusai,* the pen name he presented to Tesshu.

天地玄黃
宇宙洪荒
日月盈昃
辰宿列張
寒來暑往
秋收冬藏

書法入門之式一札
始而就書法入門之時正心潔齋
謹之御傳授相請之事
誓約
一　入木道口傳手授之旨縱令雖爲
親戚同心一切不可論說事
一　不受誓傳之許狀修行未熟之中
猥致傳授間敷事
右此條々自今以後堅致守持
候者也萬一於違犯者可蒙筆
硯童子之御罰者也仍而誓約
如件
武州
小野鐵太承
嘉永三庚戌年三月朔日　橘高歩
一高岩佐善倫先生
机下

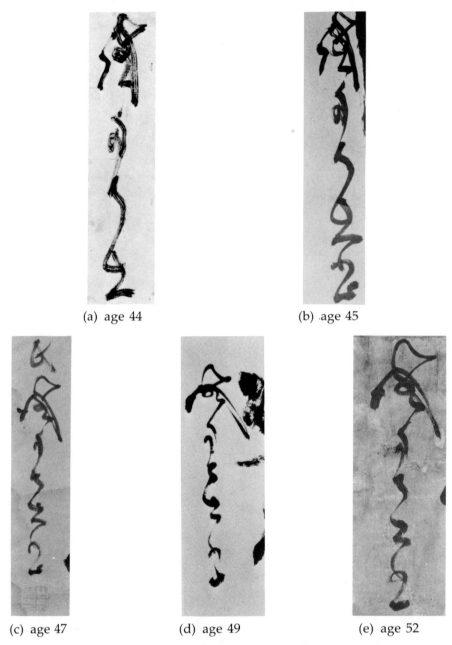

(a) age 44   (b) age 45

(c) age 47   (d) age 49   (e) age 52

If it is true that calligraphy reproduces the line of the heart, then the depth of a practitioner's enlightenment should be evident in the brush-strokes. Compare (a) Tesshu's signature at age forty-four with (b) his signature at age forty-five, a few months after his enlightenment. Each year thereafter, the deepening of Tesshu's enlightenment is reflected in the purer and purer clarity of the ink, (c)–(e). (This subject is covered in greater detail in *Zen and the Art of Calligraphy*, Routledge & Kegan Paul, 1983).

screens, made several thousand full-size (110″ × 28″) sheets for do-
nors to the Tesshuji reconstruction fund, brushed 101,000 pieces in
an eight-month period to pay for the construction of Zensho-an,
and, in the final five months of his life when he was supposedly "retired," he inscribed 40,000 fans to raise money for the construction
of a martial arts hall. Tesshu averaged an incredible five hundred
sheets a day; in a pinch he could turn out a thousand (the record
was 1,300). This is the number of *finished* pieces for sale or on special
request, and does not include spoiled or practice sheets. In addition
to all of this, Tesshu completed over a hundred volumes of *shakyo*
(sutra-copying).

On those occasions when Tesshu needed to brush a large
amount of calligraphy in a short time, he would begin right after
morning kendo practice. Five or six assistants would prepare the
ink, set up the paper, dry the finished sheets, and so on, while
Tesshu wielded the brush. Except for a few minutes' break to have a
simple meal of rice and pickled plums, Tesshu would continue well
past midnight. "Gather all things in heaven and earth in your brush
and you will never tire," Tesshu told his disciples as they dropped,
one by one, of exhaustion.

Moneylenders frequently took payment in pieces of calligraphy.
One creditor, who had traveled some distance to collect, was requested to stay over until Tesshu could arrange for the "payment."
Three days later, the creditor returned home with three thousand
made-to-order pieces. Other creditors considered Tesshu's exquis-
itely brushed I.O.U.'s more valuable than the debt and never tried to
collect.

Tesshu's calligraphy was in such demand that to maintain order
his disciples had to hand out numbers to the scores of people who
came daily to ask for a piece. One day his disciples were so angered
by a butcher's request for a signboard they refused to let him in.
Tesshu overheard the commotion and came out. "If it helps his business, that will be fine," he lectured his disciples sternly. "My calligraphy is not for sale, nor is it a commodity to be bartered; anyone

Tiger and dragon. These two fabulous animals represent the workings of the universe. The tiger (*left*) is identified with the yin principle while the dragon (*right*) symbolizes the yang principle. Portrayed together, they stand for the harmonious union of opposites—male-female, light-dark, spring-autumn, east-west. The *bokki*, the ki in the ink, is overwhelming; the two characters appear as if they might leap off the paper any second.

This piece is apparently one of 40,000 fans Tesshu brushed during the last five months of his life to raise money for a kendo hall. According to Zensho-an tradition, it was written just a few days before his death. It reads:

Temple Bell—
The pure tone
Of the bell
Lifts the clouds of illusion
Of those who
Clearly hear it.

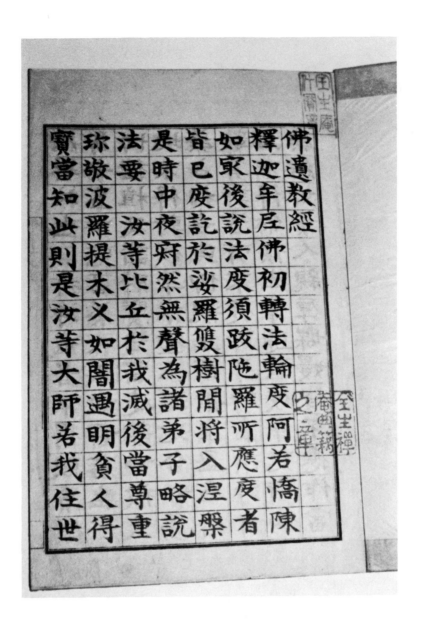

佛遺教經

釋迦牟尼佛初轉法輪度阿若憍陳
如家後說法度須跋陀羅所應度者
皆已度訖於娑羅雙樹間將入涅槃
是時中夜寂然無聲為諸弟子略說
法要汝等比丘於我滅後當尊重
珍敬波羅提木叉如闇遇明貧人得
寶當知此則是汝等大師若我住世

Tesshu's shakyo of the *Sutra of Bequeathed Teaching*. In this
sample, we can sense Tesshu's divine brush. In addition to
being perfectly formed, razor sharp in execution, the
characters are suffused with spiritual force. Each one is indeed
a new Buddha. (Unfortunately, most of Tesshu's shakyo
perished in one of the Zensho-an fires.)

who comes here with a request, regardless of what it is, should not be turned away." Even today there is a magnificent "Tesshu Soba" signboard hanging over a Tokyo noodleshop. A theater owner asked Tesshu for a suitable inscription for his enormous new eighty-four-foot-long curtain. Tesshu thought for a moment, took up a man-sized brush, and wrote in huge characters: "Ever a Full House."

Although there was no charge for Tesshu's calligraphy, most (but not all) petitioners had the common courtesy to bring something in return, either a gift or money. Whenever Tesshu received a money envelope he placed it, unopened, in a special box. If a needy person appeared, Tesshu would rummage through the box and pull out the necessary amount. The sale of Tesshu's calligraphy raised a fortune for others (including forgers), but not a yen for himself.

Tesshu's sword was life-giving; his brush was that of a Bodhisattva. Each time Tesshu brushed a piece, he would recite this one of the four Great Vows: "Sentient beings are innumerable, I vow to save them all." When a friend commented, "You sure have written a lot of pieces," Tesshu replied, "I've just begun. It will take a long time to reach thirty-five million"—the population of Japan at that time. Thus, calligraphy for Tesshu was a form of skillful means, a vehicle to guide and support others on the way to salvation.

Two years prior to his death, Tesshu announced his intention to copy the entire Buddhist canon. "Even if you live to be a hundred, you could not possibly copy more than half the canon," a friend remarked. "Why are you starting now?"

"What!" Tesshu exclaimed. "When I finish doing the entire canon in block characters, I plan to write it again in cursive script." Tesshu read his friend's mind. "No, I'm not crazy. I'll soon be exchanging this shit-bag [i.e., body] for another, so I'll be able to continue this project. Sooner or later, somewhere, someplace, I'll finish."

"Won't copying the entire canon be a great hardship?"

"Not at all. I only copy one page at a time."

Mice, once deathly afraid of Tesshu's demon zazen, now sported

This page, When a Chinese emperor asked a renowned calligrapher how to hold the brush he was told:

> If your mind is correct, the brush will be correct (*Kokoro tadashikereba sunawachi fude tadashi*). This holds true for any of the Ways. If one's mind is crooked or warped, so will be one's technique. When a calligrapher writes "no-mindedly" in the here and now, the brush strokes are vibrant; if one is distracted or full of delusion, the lines will be dead no matter how well they are constructed.

Next page, An example of Tesshu's *kaisho*, block-style calligraphy. The gist of the piece's contents, a quotation of the Chinese sage Sotoba (Su Tung Po):

> Maturity is required to properly compose characters. That is, one must ride the waves of divine energy. When one's thoughts are thus collected, calligraphy is a true pleasure. These days, however, people consider brushwork to be a burden and rarely enjoy writing. This occurs because the teaching of the great Chinese calligraphers has been ignored. They told us, "Learning calligraphy is like shooting rapids; every ounce of one's physical and mental energy must be utilized. Do not separate yourself from the ancient Ways." I have been pondering this sage advice for more than forty years. How about you?

作字要手熟則神氣完實而有餘韻于靜中自是

一樂事然常患少暇豈干其所樂常不足耶自蘇于美

死遂覺筆法中絕近年蔡君謨獨步當世住々謙讓不肯

主盟往年予嘗戲謂君謨言學書如訴急流用盡氣力不

離舊處君謨頗諾以為能取譬今思此語已四十餘年

意如何哉

錄蘇東坡與蔡君謨論書記　山岡鐵舟

Folding screen calligraphy of the *i-ro-ha*, the Japanese syllabary.
Kobo Daishi, popularly credited with the invention of this *kana*
script, arranged the fifty-one syllables into this Buddhist poem:

The colorful [flowers] are
    fragrant
But they must fall;
Who in this world of ours
Can live forever?

Today, cross over the deep
    mountains
Of life's illusions,
And there will be no more
    shallow dreaming,
No more intoxication.

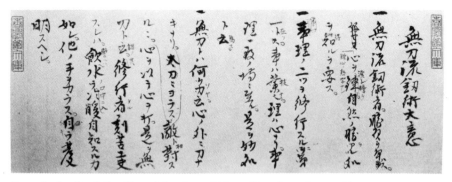

Rough draft of the *True Meaning of Muto Ryu Swordsmanship*.

on his lap and shoulders as he created a new Buddha with each character during his shakyo. Tesshu continued his shakyo until the day before his death; even in that extremity, the characters were perfectly formed with a brush that was divine.

Tesshu's advice to his calligraphy students was the same he gave his kendo trainees: stick to the fundamentals for at least three years—forget about developing individual style at first, concentrating on brushing single strokes and the *i-ro-ha*, the Japanese ABC. Thereafter, a minimum of ten years should be spent copying the classics of Chinese calligraphy. Tesshu especially recommended O Gishu; no matter how difficult it may seem, he told his students, imitate the best right from the start because that is the only way to learn. Tesshu spent twenty years copying the classics of Chinese calligraphy and countless hours contemplating the works of Japanese Zen masters—Daito, Muso, Ikkyu, Rikyu, Sesshu, Musashi, Takuan, Fugai, Hakuin, Suio, Taigado, Sengai—before creating his own unique style.

In calligraphy no less than in swordsmanship, externals must ultimately be transcended. After outlining his elaborate preparations, his careful selection of instruments and paper, and his special techniques, a noted calligrapher asked Tesshu the method he followed.

"No method."

"I don't understand."

"Which do you think is the better carpenter: one who can only work with exactly the right tools, or one who can make do with whatever is on hand?"

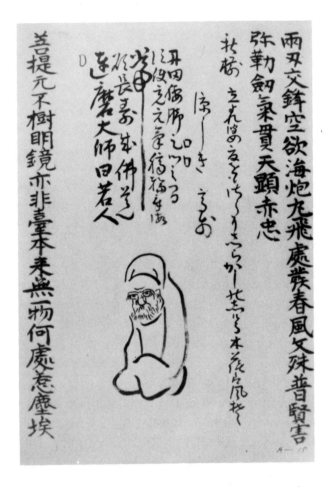

Page from Tesshu's notebook. Even on his scratch pads, Tesshu's calligraphy is extraordinarily well-composed and full of ki.

Next page, Record of Tesshu's seals. The inscription on the top, "Sincerity is god-like," was calligraphed by Yamamoto Gempo Roshi, one of the outstanding roshis of the twentieth century. Following his retirement as Abbot of Myoshinji, Gempo lived at Zensho-an for a time (one of his disciples was chief priest there).

至誠如神

玄峰

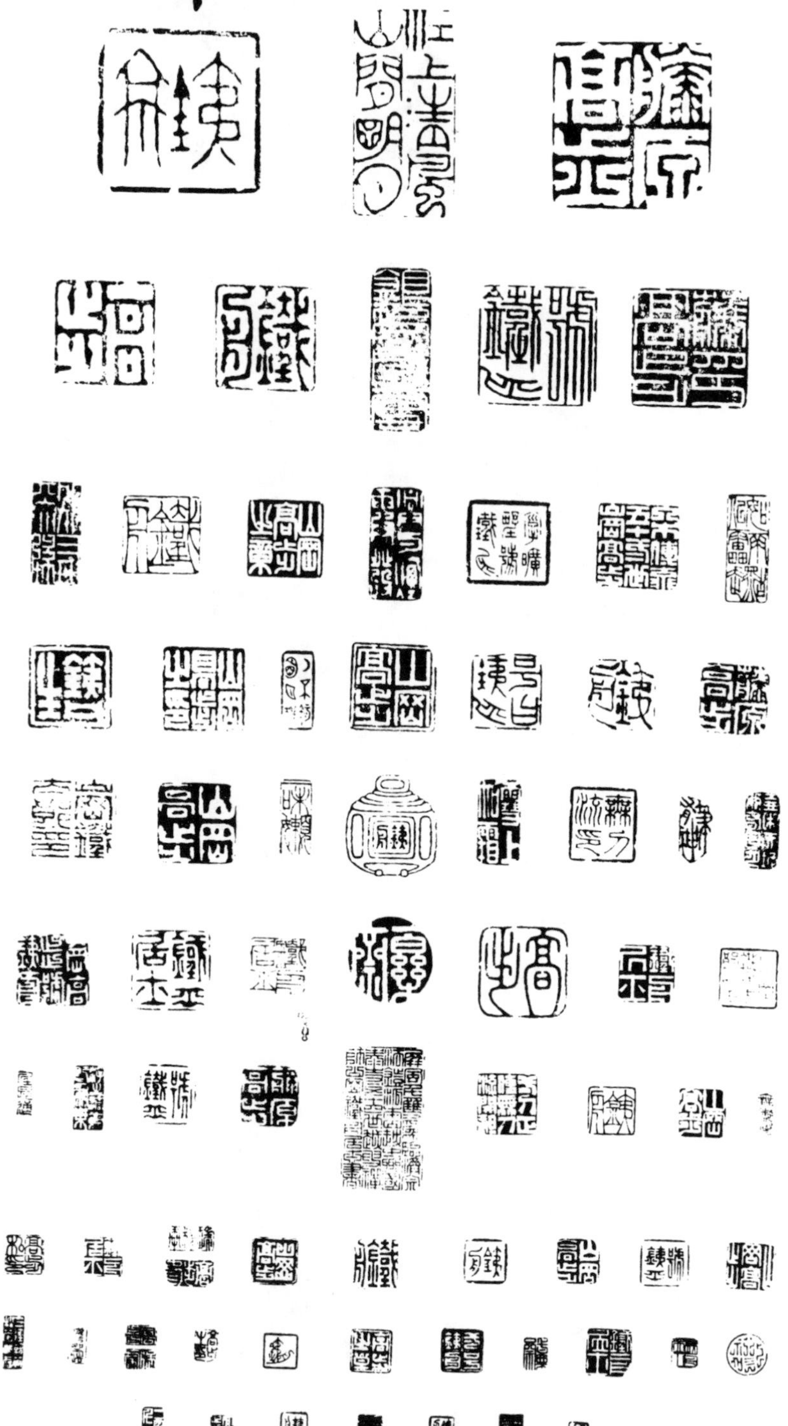

In the Far East, no clear
distinction is made between
calligraphy and painting.
Left, Bamboo. *Right*, Two pines
with poem:

A visit to
The ancient capital of Nara:
All that remains
Is the sound of the
Wind in the pines.

Wild chrysanthemums with Chinese verse:

These pale chrysanthemums are in
The fields for all to take note of
But no one comes
To appreciate them and
Their marvelous fragrance fades.

A word on Tesshu's art. Needless to say, not every one of the million works Tesshu brushed in the final eight years of his life is a masterpiece—he once joked that he was a wall painter rather than a calligrapher—and many were obviously dashed off in a frenzy of Zen enthusiasm; still, there is not a trace of stagnation or a taint of worldliness in even the most hurried pieces. Nor are there any poorly constructed characters. In his day Tesshu had many jealous critics, but not one of them was able to fault his composition—his characters were technically perfect, mastered during the long years of copying classical models.

Wonderfully unconstrained, his paintings too are a joy to contemplate, and has anyone brushed better Zen cartoons? As a master of *sho*, the highest of all art forms, Tesshu's calligraphy is indeed that of an ascending dragon.

飲中八仙歌

知章騎馬似乘船　眼花落井水底眠
汝陽三斗始朝天　道逢麴車口流涎　恨不移封向酒泉
左相日興費萬錢　飲如長鯨吸百川　銜杯樂聖稱避賢
宗之瀟灑美少年　舉觴白眼望青天　皎如玉樹臨風前
蘇晉長齋繡佛前　醉中往往愛逃禪
李白一斗詩百篇　長安市上酒家眠　天子呼來不上船　自稱臣是酒中仙
張旭三杯草聖傳　脫帽露頂王公前　揮毫落紙如雲煙
焦遂五斗方卓然　高談雄辯驚四筵

Chinese characters for *The Eight Immortals of the Winecup*. See Tesshu's version on pages 108–109 and translation on page 110.

Omori Sogen uses Tesshu's calligraphy of Tu Fu's poem "The Eight Immortals of the Winecup" as the copy book for calligraphy practice in his Tesshu Society.

THE EIGHT IMMORTALS OF THE WINECUP

Chi-chang sways to and fro on his horse
    as if he were on a reeling ship;
Should he fall bleary-eyed into a well,
    he would probably fall fast asleep on its bottom.
Ju-yang the prince needs three gallons
    first thing in the morning;
How his mouth waters when the brewer's cart passes by;
    too bad he can't be Lord of the Wine Spring.
Li the minister spends thousands to indulge his daily habit,
    gulping rivers of wine like a great whale;
Cherishing his cup, he takes pleasure in wisdom water
    while promising to retire from office as soon as he can.
Tsung-chi is a handsome youth
    who disdains the base;
Holding his beloved cup he fixes his gaze on heaven,
    resplendent as a jade tree in a gentle wind.
Su Chin the monk
    chants before his Buddha image,
But often breaks off his meditation
    to go on a spree.
Li Po gets a hundred poems out of one gallon;
    he naps in a wine shop in Chang-an
Refusing to board the Imperial Barge when the emperor beckons:
    "Please, Your Majesty, I am an Immortal of Wine."
Chang Hsu the reknowned calligrapher has three cups
    and he is ready to go;
Ignoring court etiquette he removes his hat
    and dashes off a masterpiece.
Chao Sui downs five gallons
    and fills the banquet hall
With marvelous speech,
    his eloquence the wonder of all.

5

THE THREE SHU

Tesshu was the junior member of the *Bakumatsu no sanshu*, "The Three Shu of the Bakumatsu Era." The Three Shu—Katsu Kaishu, Takahashi Deishu, and Yamaoka Tesshu—were Zen statesmen, public servants of the highest order indifferent to money, power, and personal glory. Each took the character, *shu* (boat) for the second element of his pen name: *kai-shu*, "ocean-boat," maneuvers through the vast sea; *dei-shu*, "mud-boat," rock hard on land, slowly dissolves without a trace when set in water; *tetsu-shu*, "iron-boat," is the marvelous ship of Layman P'ang:

> To foster life everything must be killed:
> Once all is destroyed, you can dwell at ease.
> If you understand this inner meaning,
> An iron boat will float across the water.

Katsu Kaishu was born in 1823 to an impoverished, low-ranking samurai family in Edo. As a child, Kaishu acted as playmate-attendant for one of the Shogun's sons and received the standard samurai education in Chinese classics, calligraphy, and poetry. Otani Nobutomo, thirteenth Headmaster of the Jikishinkage Ryu, was Kaishu's first swordsmanship teacher, and at age sixteen, Kaishu became the disciple of the Confucian scholar-swordsman Shimada

Toranosuke. Shimada advised Kaishu, "If you want to master the secrets of swordsmanship, study Zen. That is the quickest way."

For the next four years, Kaishu divided his time between the meditation hall and the kendo gym; every night he sequestered himself in a mountain shrine, alternating periods of swinging his sword with periods of meditation right up to daybreak. Kaishu often commented that these years of severe training in swordsmanship and Zen enabled him to face unflinchingly the many hardships and life-threatening events of his later life—always by keeping his blade firmly sheathed in its scabbard and repelling every challenge with the power of a "gentleman's sword." Kaishu received a Jikishinkage Ryu teacher's license when he was twenty-one years old, but realized that Japan would no longer be able to defend itself with swords alone.

Consequently, Kaishu decided to study European military science and he mastered Dutch, then the *lingua franca* of western learning. Kaishu did not neglect his Oriental studies, however; one of his teachers told him, "Now that modern science is becoming established all over the world, both easterners and westerners must not be allowed to forget the teachings of the great sages of the Orient. Study well eastern thought and western technology in order to be a beacon for your fellow man." Kaishu's manner of study was to read western language books in the morning, Chinese classics during the day, and Japanese works in the evening. Penniless like so many of the samurai of that time, Kaishu had to limit himself to one meal a day and his desk doubled as his bed cover. After most of the boards in the ceiling of his house had gone for firewood, Kaishu borrowed a rare Dutch book and made two handwritten copies, one for himself and the other to be sold. Despite his poverty, Kaishu never complained or looked back on this trying period with regret. "Adversity makes the man," was the samurai creed and Kaishu's personal motto was: "Detached from self, in harmony with others, settled during calm, resolute during action, composed in thought, and firm during setbacks."

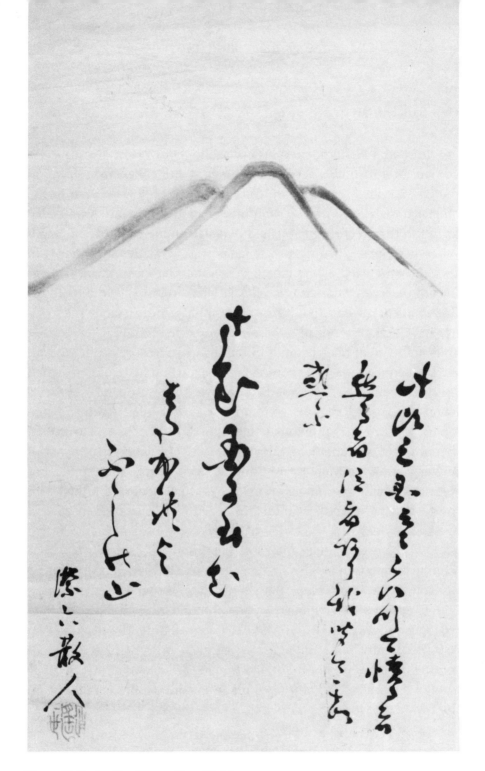

Three Fujis by the Three Shu: Kaishu.

These days people grumble about the Three Countries [Russia, France, Germany], and many are resentful, anxious and upset; when I hear such nonsense I become perplexed—answer the Three Countries with the spirit of Mt. Fuji.

In 1850, Kaishu opened his own school of western learning. As a result of a favorably received letter containing Kaishu's views on the coastal defenses of Japan, the Shogunate appointed him to the official translation bureau in Shimoda. In 1855, Kaishu was transferred to the recently established Naval Training Institute in Nagasaki where he studied naval science with several Dutch captains. In 1860, Kaishu acted as the Japanese commander of the *Kenrin Maru*, the ship carrying Japan's first official delegation to the United States. (In America, it seems that Kaishu was chiefly impressed by the manner in which all types of classes of people freely mingled together and by the great respect and kindness shown toward women.) Following a four-and-a-half-month stay, Kaishu and his group returned to Japan where he continued his efforts to develop his country's naval capacity—Kaishu is sometimes referred to as "Father of the Japanese Navy." As previously mentioned, he and Tesshu arranged the peaceful surrender of Edo Castle and the smooth transfer of power during the Meiji Restoration of 1868. A prominent official of the new Meiji government, Kaishu eventually became Minister of the Navy and served as Councillor of State. Kaishu died in 1899 at age seventy-seven.

Kaishu was among Japan's earliest internationalists. He was a member of modern Japan's first delegation to a western country, and his son, who spent more than ten years studying in the United States, appears to have been Japan's first overseas scholar (*ryugaku sei*). Kaishu was deeply involved in foreign affairs throughout his career, frequently being called on to negotiate with the likes of Townsend Harris, Harry Smith-Parkes, Ernest Satow, and a host of other foreign emissaries. Kaishu once made this interesting comment on the conduct of foreign affairs:

> When I was young I learned that the secret of swordsmanship was to keep your mind clear and serene like a bright mirror (*meikyo-shisui*); the secret of successfully conducting foreign affairs is no different. Most diplomats plan in advance how to react to certain situations and set inflexible standards of response. That is a great mistake. It is better not to have some particular scheme

in mind and not to stick to abstract principles. Abandon all limiting ideas and do not allow illusions and misconceptions to cloud one's vision. Keep the mind clear and serene like a bright mirror, and regardless of what occurs one will be able to deal with it in a natural, suitable manner.

Kaishu believed that one should follow such an approach in all aspects of life—while conducting foreign affairs, while swinging a sword, while sitting on a cushion.

Kaishu's Zen teaching may be summarized like this:

Sit and forget everything. When there is not a single thing in your mind, any circumstance can be freely dealt with. If you are full of anxiety and constantly fret about this and that, you will never be able to handle anything well. What a human being needs, above all, is daily physical and mental training, constant forging and deepening of the spirit. Samurai were trained as a matter of course to live simply with a minimum of possessions. It is much better to be free of attachment to things and events; when one has attained a high level of insight, he is unconcerned with the ceaseless flow of activities and objects.

Kaishu was not just a master of statesmanship, kendo, and Zen. In addition to his legal wife, he had at least five other companions over the years, fathering a minimum of nine children. It is said that at the time of his death in his late seventies, Kaishu was living with six young women.

Takahashi Deishu, the least well-known of the Three Shu due to his early retirement from public affairs, was born in 1835. His Edo samurai family was somewhat better off than that of Kaishu's (Tesshu's Ono clan was the highest ranking of the three); Deishu was born a Yamaoka but adopted Takahashi, his mother's maiden name, in his teens in order to preserve that family line. The Takahashi-Yamaoka clan had produced a number of outstanding martial artists, the family specialty being spear fighting. At a tender age, Deishu began practice of that art, initially under his grandfather and then with his older brother, Seizan. After Seizan's untimely death at age twenty-seven, Deishu took over the training hall while Tesshu married his sister and assumed the Yamaoka name.

Although Deishu apparently never formally studied Zen as did the other two Shu, he once had a run-in with a Zen priest who gave him a valuable hint. Deishu was visiting a temple in Ueno on family business and happened to boast to the priest there how skillful he was with the spear.

"Is that so?" remarked the priest. "How about a demonstration? Do you think you can touch me with your weapon?"

Angered by the priest's cavalier disregard of his reputation, Deishu grabbed a laundry pole, prepared to make short work of the monk. To his consternation, Deishu got nowhere near the priest who deftly avoided every thrust. Deishu was forced to concede defeat and beseeched the priest, "What school do you profess? Please teach me the principles of your Ryu."

"I belong to the 'Mountains are high, rivers are long' Ryu. It is also known as the 'Eyes horizontal, nose vertical' or the 'Willows are green, flowers are red' School."

"What do you mean?" a confused Deishu asked.

"Figure it out for yourself," the Zen priest told him.

Deishu also had a special relationship with a Zen-like Jodo Shinshu priest named Rinzui. Rinzui enjoyed confronting Deishu with such koan-like sayings as, "Something must act as nothing; nothing must act as something. Shatter both ends and drop off the middle!" Deishu pondered Rinzui's riddles while he practiced with his spear. One night after three years of puzzling over the great matter of life and death, Deishu dreamed he saw his dead brother, Seizan. The two engaged in several matches, Seizan imparted the secrets of the spear to him, and Deishu had a profound realization. Following this experience, Deishu was said to be invincible with the spear.

After being appointed official instructor of spear fighting to the Shogun, Deishu gradually became more involved in politics. He served as a government representative in Ise for a time, but was falsely accused of plotting a rebellion and placed under house ar-

Deishu. The Chinese poem on the right reads:

> No mountain rivals this lotus
>   peak at dusk,
> Soaring in solitary splendor
>   above the clouds.
> Its beauty is not easily
>   portrayed—
> Deep purples and bright reds
> disappear in the
>   fading light.

The Japanese poems on the left run:

> The glories of
> The Three Imperial Treasures
> Seem to sparkle
> All over the world reflected
> By Fuji the Sacred Mountain.

> Place it in the
> Palm of your hand
> And show everyone
> Fuji in spring.

rest. Upon enactment of the Meiji Restoration in 1868, Deishu retired from public life. Deishu had a much closer relationship to Yoshinobu, the last Tokugawa Shogun, than either Kaishu or Tesshu, and he felt that he should follow his lord into seclusion when Yoshinobu was forced to resign. Even though Deishu was nominated for several important posts by the Meiji government, he lived quietly out of the limelight (supported by Tesshu), devoting himself to poetry, calligraphy, and painting until his death in 1903 at age sixty-nine.

Deishu may have exchanged his spear for a brush, but his attitude remained the same: full-spirited utilization of the body and mind without the slightest break in concentration. Deishu once made this revealing observation about calligraphy: "Even if you are too busy with everyday affairs to pick up a brush, you still can improve your calligraphy by improving your mind. On no account should you neglect your duties to practice brushwork. Any work that is well done will improve your calligraphy by strengthening your spirit. No ancient worthy ever believed that the practice of calligraphy was limited to the actual time one is free enough to write."

Regarding Zen, Deishu had this to say: "If a fine sword is not constantly polished, it will never show its luster. If you don't practice, you will never be able to master universals and particulars. Plenty of people can talk about Zen but not many can live it. Get to work!" He said on another occasion:

> If a fellow such as I wanted to attain enlightenment, this is what he would do: First, he would grab Emma, the King of Hell, by the seat of his pants and fling him to the ground; then he would whip Emma's minions into submission; after conquering all regions of the netherworld, he would head directly for the Pure Land, scattering the Arhats and Bodhisattvas until he met up with Buddha himself; without hesitation, he would force Shakyamuni off the Lotus Throne and install himself there as the only honored one in heaven and earth!

When Deishu learned that his thick-headed brother-in-law Tesshu had attained enlightenment, he slapped his knee and exclaimed, "It's about time!"

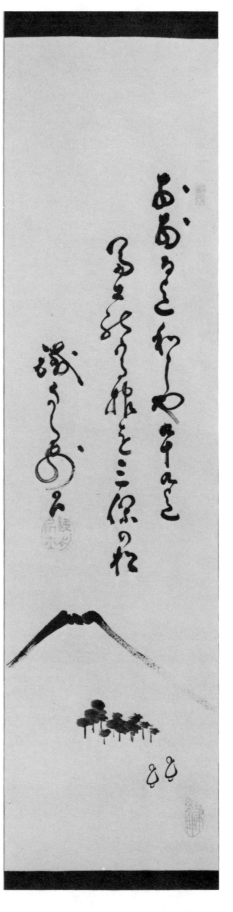

Tesshu.

> You'll reach a hundred, I'll
>   reach ninety-nine;
> The peak of Mt. Fuji, the
>   pines of Miho

This splendid painting is
perhaps Tesshu's finest,
certainly one of the best
Zenga ever brushed.

6

TESSHU'S WRITINGS

A man of few words, Tesshu's own writings are short and to the point. Regarding the personal behavior of his trainees, for example, there were only two tenets: "No stealing and no lying," and these rules were not posted until after someone's watch disappeared. Similarly, most of his writings were composed in response to a specific problem or request. The only lengthy pieces are Tesshu's copies of Itto Ryu *mokuroku*, "catalogue of techniques."

Many of the writings attributed to Tesshu are, in fact, not from his brush. Near the end of the Meiji era, a fellow named Abe Masato published *Tesshu Genko Roku*, a purported collection of Tesshu's essays. Although most of those essays are spurious, riddled with contradictions and impossibilities, a few of them—e.g., "Swordsmanship and the Principles of Zen" (*Kenpo to Zenri*)—have had wide circulation, causing much confusion. Likewise, the reliability of the large number of "recorded by a disciple" pieces is in question; however, I have included excerpts from this group that seem to represent correctly Tesshu's thinking. Almost all of the material presented here is translated directly from Tesshu's originals preserved in the Shumpukan Bunko.

無刀流釼法者事理一致ヲ修行スルニアリ蓋古来ヨリ諸流ノ始祖剏苦精練シ各目巽明スルニヨリ竟ニ其流名ヲ立シモノナリ

Opening and ending
sections of "Rules for
the Practice of Muto
Ryu Swordsmanship"
in Tesshu's own hand.

刀見ル処已足ニ異ナリ外見ノ體裁ニ不拘真理自然ニ勝ヲ治メラ無形ノ地ヲ占ルモノナリ故ニ此道ヲ修セント欲セハ初心ノ者ヲテ力門ニ

スルヲ禁ス何ントナレハ将ニ其體ヲ備ヘントセシヲ破レハナリ柳無刀流ハ子テ力巽明スル処ミシテ事理一致ノ秘訣ナリ其教ニ至ハ古傳ヲ以テ

入リ勇悍不退ノ志ヲ勵マシ苦修鍛練スル時ハ三年ミシテ流義ノ體ヲ備ヘン其體ヲ備ヘサルニ即今流行ノ演武場ニ行ヲ猥ニ試合

ス入門ノ士此規則ヲ遵守ス可シ
明治十三年三月三十日
無刀流開祖山岡鐵太郎

Rules for the Practice of Muto Ryu Swordsmanship
(I)

Muto Ryu swordsmanship is the practice of unifying particulars and universals.[1] From the past, the founders of every school discovered this principle through hard, ceaseless training, making it the core of their respective traditions. These days, most schools have become lax and no longer observe the proper methods. In general, the bamboo sword is now used exclusively for conducting contests. This occurs because few know the real meaning of swordsmanship, most chase after inferior techniques, and the schools themselves merely maintain appearances. Such swordsmen may fare well on a battlefield through good fortune but theirs is not a decisive victory. My interpretation is different from the prevailing standards. By not clinging to externals and styles, true victory is naturally[2] attained as the swordsman reaches a state of no-form. One who wishes to follow this path and enters my school must practice intensely with great determination; during the initial three-year training period the principles of my school must be firmly grasped. In order to avoid confusion, new trainees are prohibited from witnessing other schools' demonstrations or from participating in open contests. If this is not enforced, the system of training will be destroyed. Within the principles of my Muto Ryu lie the secrets of unifying particulars and universals. This teaching has an ancient tradition and all my trainees must faithfully observe these rules.

March 30, 1880[3]

Enlightenment through the Way of the Sword

Study hard and all things can be accomplished; give up and you will amount to nothing.

When I was nine years old, I took a keen interest in swordsmanship and began study with Kusumi Kantekisai of the Shinkage Ryu. Later, I entered the dojo of Inoue Kiyotora of the Hokuto Itto Ryu and broadened my practice by engaging in thousands of contests with swordsmen of all styles. For more than twenty years, I trained relentlessly without attaining the peace of mind I sought. In vain, I searched everywhere for a truly enlightened master of the Way of the Sword; then I met Asari Matashichiro of the Itto Ryu. Asari was the second son of Nakanishi Chubee and successor of the Ito Ittosai tradition of swordsmanship. Since he was a real master, I eagerly applied for a contest with him. Asari was different from any other swordsman I had ever faced—flexible on the outside, diamond hard on the inside. His intense spiritual concentration enabled him to secure victory before his opponent made a move. He was truly an enlightened master. Thereafter, I faced him countless times, but regardless of how hard I tried, I found no way to defeat him. Every day after regular training with various swordsmen, I dreamed that Asari was standing before me like a mountain. It was impossible for me to strike back or to drive that vision away.

Then early in the morning of March 30, 1880, as I imagined myself crossing swords with Asari, the vision vanished and I attained the ultimate state of no-enemy. I quickly went to Asari's dojo to test my attainment. He told me,"You have realized the marvelous principle." Based on that awakening I subsequently established a system I call the Muto Ryu. When questioned about such matters, the ancient worthies would tell their disciples: "If you make an effort, there will be insight; hard training surely leads to the ultimate principles." Students of the Way: never stop practicing!

> For years I forged my spirit through the study of
>   swordsmanship,
> Confronting every challenge steadfastly.
> The walls surrounding me suddenly crumbled;
> Like pure dew reflecting the world in crystal clarity,
>   total awakening has now come.

> Using thought to analyze reality is illusion;
> If preoccupied with victory and defeat all will be lost.
> The secret of swordsmanship?
> Lightning slashes the spring wind!

June, 1880[4]

The True Meaning of Muto Ryu Swordsmanship

1. Swordsmen of the Muto Ryu do not seek supremacy through contests; they clarify their minds through diligent training and attain victory naturally.

2. "Particular" and "universal" are the two aspects of practice. "Particular" is technique, "universal" is Mind. Where particular and universal are harmonized we find the world of marvelous[5] activity.

3. What is "no sword?" Outside the Mind, there is no sword. When facing an opponent, do not depend on the sword; use Mind to strike the adversary's mind. This is "no sword." Maintain this practice through earnest discipline and realize it by oneself. Do not rely on others; discover it on your own!

Muto Ryu Strategy

The Five Components:

> *Myo-ken*, Marvelous Sword
> *Zetsumyo-ken*, Exquisite Sword
> *Shin-ken*, True Sword
> *Konchichoo-ken*, Sword of the Golden-winged
>   Garuda[6] King
> *Dokumyo-ken*, Sword of Solitary Splendor

These Muto Ryu sword techniques are not for combat; they are for training the mind and polishing technique which allows natural victory to be ours. When these marvelous techniques are performed, the sword is swung [according to this principle]: "Outside the mind there is no sword; facing the enemy, no one stands before our eyes." Move freely through all dimensions and use Mind to strike mind— this is "Lightning slashes the spring wind."

The essence of swordsmanship lies in mastery of the two aspects of universal and particular. Particular refers to technique; universal refers to Mind. Once [body and mind] are polished and refined, one arrives at the marvelous state where particular and universal are unified. Continue to forge the spirit and particular and universal will ultimately be forgotten—this is "a single sword against the cold sky."[7] If you want to obtain the secrets of such wonderful techniques, drill yourself, harden yourself, undergo severe training, abandon body and mind; follow this course for years and you will naturally reach the profoundest levels. To know if water is hot or cold you must taste it yourself. In this manner, sword techniques are transmitted from mind to mind. This is Muto Ryu swordsmanship.

> Standing in the dojo of *suigetsu*,[8]
> Striking at the flowers of emptiness with a naked blade.

June, 1880

PROPER ATTITUDE FOR BEGINNING STUDENTS

Those who study swordsmanship must not get caught up with concepts of good-bad-victory-defeat during the initial years of practice. In order not to develop improper habits, strive with your entire being, forcefully and without restraint swing the sword over and over, extend yourself to the fullest, and concentrate on executing the techniques naturally. Eventually, real strength will be fostered; all stiffness will vanish and the techniques can be performed in a free-flowing manner. The opponent's movements can be detected before he strikes—one intuitively knows where to cut and any attack can be repelled. Have no confused thoughts or doubts, do not distort the techniques: without delay, train harder and harder!

THE SEVEN WAYS TO ATTAIN VICTORY

1. Suppressing the opponent's ki
2. Anticipating the attack
3. Responding to the attack
4. Holding down
5. Driving back
6. Overwhelming
7. Proper adjustment

These seven ways of attaining victory must always be kept in mind. If they are ignored, it will be difficult to have proper understanding of the Way of the Sword. If one trains aimlessly, Mind cannot develop, time is wasted, and there is useless expense of energy. Thus, I formulated these seven basic procedures at the request of Mr. Maeda and taught them to him over a seventeen-day period.

August, 1880

SHUIN TACHI

Ittosai Ito Kagehisa presented this *shuin tachi* (inscribed wooden sword) to Ono Jiroemon Tadaaki. From Tadaaki it was handed down through thirteen generations until Tetsutaro received it as a symbol of the transmission. Times have changed and true swordsmanship must be revived. I am entrusting you, Koteta, with this responsibility. You must never abandon your vow to maintain the tradition. As a tangible symbol of our school I am presenting this shuin tachi to you. Do not let worldlings or greedy people clog the True Path with weeds. It is regrettable that the essence of our Way, the unification of particular and universal, must be kept secret [to avoid misunderstanding and misuse]. If this law is not properly preserved, not only will the true face of Kagehisa be defiled; all the teachings of the various patriarchs will be lost. Since I trust you not to do such a thing, I have presented you with this sword.[7]

May 3, 1881

TRUE AND FALSE SWORDSMANSHIP

Those who correctly transmit the ultimate principles of swordsman-ship have no special technique. They attain victory by entering their adversary's favorite place. What is the enemy's "favorite place?" Whenever two swords cross, all thoughts turn toward striking the opponent. By blending one's entire body with that of the opponent, one enters the opponent's favorite place [i.e., his point of greatest strength] and thus attains "victory through true victory." For ex-ample, prior to taking something from a box, one first removes the lid, looks carefully at the contents, and ascertains what it is. This is natural victory, requiring no special technique. However, even this procedure can become either extremely easy or extremely difficult depending on the approach. Students of the Way should not look at things in such simplistic terms.

Swordsmen of other schools do not act in a natural manner. When they confront an opponent, they immediately get agitated and attempt to defeat the other swordsman through a hot-blooded frontal attack. This is a grave mistake. Those who practice in this way may be victorious in their youth when they are full of vigor and strength. However, when they no longer can depend on physical power due to age or ill health, their inadequately formed techniques will fail them—it is as if they had not studied swordsmanship at all, a needless waste of effort. This is false swordsmanship. Students of the Way must awaken to this principle while training harder and harder.

January 5, 1882

The State of No Enemy

From age nine I enjoyed the practice of swordsmanship. When I was young I thought of nothing except striking my opponent with all my might. Regardless of my position, I would swing my sword freely. I continuously practiced in that manner for ten years. Gradually, I became more skillful and was able to move freely in all directions; I was confident of victory. However, in my twenties I began fixing on my opponent's sword and lost my fluid movement. Whatever the reason, while striking at my opponent I was now perplexed, no longer possessing my former agility. Something was lacking in my practice and my training was unsatisfactory. I became determined to train harder than ever. I was twenty-eight or -nine then, in my prime; day and night I trained, endlessly facing opponents, using every ounce of my strength. At that time I was able to take the measure of a swordsman simply by looking at his posture, but that was all. Practicing for years and gaining no more than the ability to gauge another's prowess is a sorry state of affairs. Nevertheless, I knew that my struggle would eventually lead me to the right path. I would continue searching even if swordsmanship disappeared from the world and not one opponent remained. I would not stop until I finally penetrated the ultimate principle.

Year after year I practiced; on March 30, 1880, I reached the state of no-enemy. I cannot describe my great joy at that time. The traditional, rightly transmitted teaching is kind and true; there is no doubt about it. I was then forty-five years old. As I recalled my previous notions of skillfulness and ineptness, fighting and no fighting, I realized that those dichotomies have nothing to do with the opponent; all those things are creations of one's mind. If there is self, there is an enemy; if there is no self, there is no enemy. If we are enlightened to the truth of this principle, skill-ineptitude, weakness-strength, child-adult, and so on are no longer seen as two separate entities. This is: "Lovely snowflakes falling one by one nowhere else" [10]—a marvelous place.

January 8, 1882

SERENITY OF MIND

The basis of true training in swordsmanship is to forge the spirit. Our primary purpose is to face our opponents without the slightest opening (*suki*) in our defense. What is "opening?" "Opening" means wishing to strike the opponent while avoiding being struck by him. Such a thought is deluded. Originally, the mind is thought-less like a bright, unclouded mirror. However, when one delusive thought arises, a shadow appears; when a shadow appears, the mirror is clouded. When the mirror is completely clouded, nothing can be re-flected. When confronting an opponent, thoughts of striking or being struck indicate ignorance and illusion. Do not even think of standing vacantly in front of the opponent. Maintain the principle of [no-mindedly] dodging strikes and avoiding thrusts and you will lack nothing. This is a natural, marvelous principle. Do not use dis-criminatory thought and total victory will be yours. Everyone must realize this marvelous principle.

February 8, 1882

Swordsmanship consists of utilizing no-form within form to achieve victory.

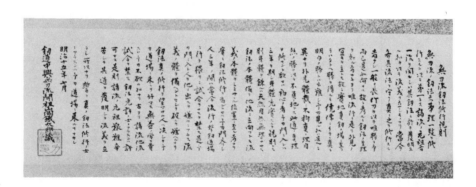

Original version of "Rules for the Practice of Muto Ryu Swordsmanship" in Tesshu's own hand.

Rules for the Practice of Muto Ryu Swordsmanship (II)

The first principle of Muto Ryu swordsmanship is the practice of unifying particulars and universals. All the founders of other schools discovered that principle of swordsmanship, making it the basis of their respective teachings. At present, there are no schools that preserve that principle by truly practicing it. In general, swordsmen today seek victory only through sword technique. The reason for this degeneration is that modern swordsmen are ignorant of the essential principles of swordsmanship: they merely follow popular trends and maintain appearances. In a real battlefield such swordsmen may win through good fortune, but theirs is not a decisive victory. My viewpoint is different. Not clinging to externals or styles, invincibility is achieved by relying on the principles of truth and natural victory. One wishing to practice this true path by entering my school must forge the body for [a minimum of] three years. Forging of the body must be carried out naturally, free of artifice or strain. While the basis of swordsmanship is being formed one is not permitted to visit other schools because that results in confusion. One who sincerely desires to practice swordsmanship and enrolls in my school will not be allowed to randomly visit other training halls or to engage swordsmen of different schools for a three-year period. It is not that I disapprove of disciples visiting other schools, but I do not want the training system broken. I do not want anyone in the training hall who does not wish to practice true swordsmanship nor do do I want to see a needless waste of effort. Traditionally, contests among beginners of different schools were prohibited; if one was not a licensed swordsman such permission was not granted. After much hardship the founders of all schools discovered this path and established their systems around it. Let it be known that those who lack conviction to practice true swordsmanship are not welcome in my dojo.

July, 1882

RETURN TO BEGINNER'S MIND

If the marvels of swordsmanship elude you, return to beginner's mind. Beginner's mind is not any "kind" of mind—striking single-mindedly without thinking of the body and moving ahead forcefully is proof that one has forgotten self. Technicians are hampered by analytic thinking. Once the obstacle of discursive thought is surmounted the marvels of swordsmanship can be appreciated. At first, it is necessary to practice with skilled swordsmen in order to discern one's inadequacies. Pursue your study to the end, awaken your irresistible force, practice ceaselessly until your heart is immovable, and then you will understand. Train until no doubts remain. Surely the time will come when the marvels are discovered.

August, 1882

THE TRIANGLE RULE OF SWORDSMANSHIP

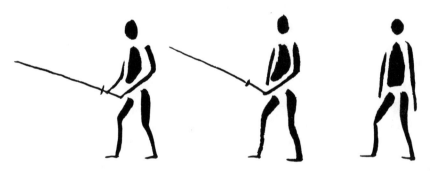

3. Triangle rule   2. Holding the sword   1. Stance

The triangle rule of swordsmanship—keeping the eyes, abdomen, and swordtip together in a triangle—must be strictly observed.

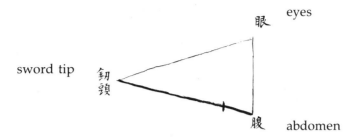

The length of a sword is determined to be ten times the width of one's hand; ten times makes it approximately one-half the length of one's body. Do not separate the three sides of the triangle—eyes, abdomen, and swordtip—when facing the opponent. Since the sword is one-half the length of both arms extended sideways, when holding a sword ten hand-breadths in length slightly lean the entire body toward the opponent [as shown in 3]. From ancient times, this has been called *Tenshin Shoden*, "Heavenly Truth Rightly Transmitted." The triangle rule is the basis of Tenshin Shoden.

Tenshin Shoden

All those learning swordsmanship in this school must make this triangle rule the basis of their study. Phenomena possess form and thus can be utilized; if there was no form, there could be no utilization. Swordsmanship is no different. Once form is mastered, we know how to make use of its principles. The triangle rule must be strictly adhered to and practiced; then it will be possible to grasp the inner teaching that form and function are not two. Study hard! Study hard!

March 30, 1883

NOTICE POSTED IN THE SHUMPUKAN DOJO

From ancient times, the standard sword length has been set at ten hand-breadths. Ten hand-breadths is approximately one-half the length of the body. Hence, when swords are crossed the space between the two opponents is twenty hand-breadths, i.e., one body length. There is also a sword eight hand-breadths long. Because this sword is so short greater attention and sharper focus is necessary when confronting an opponent. In the past, swordsmen followed this standard approach and all schools used bamboo swords ten hand-breadths or less in length.

During the Tempo era [1830–43] a fellow named Oishi Susumu of the Yanagigawa clan roamed the country, challenging various masters with his five-foot long sword. Oishi came to Edo to storm the dojos there and had a contest with Chiba Shusaku. When Oishi displayed his five-foot sword, Chiba countered by placing a huge wooden lid around the hilt of his sword as a guard. Some may enjoy playing with such toys, but our swordsmanship is not like that. Unfortunately, these days virtually all schools have fallen under the spell of such shenanigans; because hardly anyone is aware of traditional standards, the use of excessively long swords is now the custom. This lack of study and proper knowledge is indeed lamentable. Anyone with at least a little background in swordsmanship should know better than to engage in such ostentation. Since present day instructors like to show off with gimmicks while avoiding real man-to-man contests, it is no surprise abuses occur. All those who wish to restore the Way of the Sword must construct their bamboo swords according to the ancient standards, wielding it as if it were a live blade. Future generations too must preserve this standard.

September 14, 1883

ANCIENT TRADITIONS

Our nation has a well-established tradition regarding the length of a sword. All the founders of the various schools of swordsmanship followed the ancient standard which I believe must be restored. Recently, I have stated my views on the matter of proper sword length, and it is more than simply a private opinion. Ever since Oishi Susumu of the Yanagigawa Clan began using a long sword during the Tempo era, the schools have lost sight of the merits of a short sword, gradually abandoning the traditions of their predecessors. Use of a long sword is now nearly universal—the Shinkage Ryu, the Shinkei Ryu, the Munen Ryu, the Itto Ryu, and all the rest have capitulated. It is clear to me that use of a long sword is contrary to the dictates of the patriarchs. Modern practitioners are the heirs of Oishi [not the past masters]. From childhood, I studied various systems and have been practicing for nearly forty years. The true meaning of swordsmanship suddenly dawned on me and I subsequently opened the Muto Ryu. Nevertheless, I have not tampered with the tradition of Ittosai[11] or altered his teachings in the slightest. For decades, Ittosai practiced intensely at the risk of his life, kindly bestowing his great teachings to posterity. We must honor them intact. As the old saying goes, "Keep to the source and foster the Way." There may be some value in conducting matches, but if the traditional teaching is not maintained it will be impossible to attain the ultimate principles no matter how long one trains. Present day sports contests depend on the use of long swords; that is not the true Way of practice. I beseech all students of swordsmanship to reflect deeply on this matter.

UPON THE ESTABLISHMENT OF THE JAPAN SWORDSMANSHIP ASSOCIATION

In order to be successful in a contest, swordsmen must know how to strike the opponent. However, that technique is extremely subtle and difficult to master. There is this teaching: "Thirst for victory leads to defeat; not tiring of defeat leads to victory." Those ignorant of that principle fritter away years of training without realizing a thing. Wasted effort harms everyone. Generally swordsmen rely exclusively on technique to wage their battles. That is a mistake. Prior to drilling with others, drill yourself. Forging of the spirit and self-control is the only path. This is the principle of "All things return to the One." To attain it, work hard and concentrate the spirit— such is the teaching of our predecessors. At the request of Mr. Fuku I have composed, in light of my own experience, this brief message on the occasion of the establishment of the Japan Swordsmanship Association.

September, 1883

THE SINGLE SOURCE OF SUBSTANCE AND FUNCTION

All things in the universe have substance and function. Our swordsmanship is no different. If there is no substance, nothing can be acted upon or carried through. What is "substance?" "The inner quiet of the mind, free of individual failings." If there is no such quiet, the enemies of the spirit cannot be overcome and no freedom can be attained. Therefore, clearly illumine the nature of truth and falsehood according to substance.

Recklessly striking and thrusting will not prevail over an opponent's mind. The lack of calm in one's own heart causes agitation to arise from all quarters, thus preventing mastery of the opponent. Know that this occurs for no other reason but one's lack of substance. Depending on chance and lucky breaks to win never results in true victory. Reflect upon this and it will become clear. True attainment must be accomplished within the quiet of one's mind.

If you want peace of mind, first perfect substance. If substance is not perfected, the heart will never be at rest. This is the meaning of "substance and function are one." Beginners who wish to study this path must abandon self, resolutely confront the opponent with full-spirited concentration, and act decisively like a flash of lightning, devoid of extraneous thoughts. With a sincere mind begin the quest; start each day anew and progress month by month. If you understand how to be firmly in the center of self and others, every cut will be perfectly controlled. This is termed the "interval of subtle change and natural adaptability."

Act in accordance to this principle when facing an opponent and there will be no misdirected attacks. This is called "knowing the opponent." Progress further and the opponent's relative degree of skill can be discerned immediately. This is called "knowing oneself and knowing the opponent." Advance to the final stage and the opponent's stance or position no longer has any influence. This is called "forgetting the opponent." That level of attainment cannot be described by pen or speech. Make strenuous efforts to attain these marvelous secrets.

This is the single source of substance and function, a law without the slightest weakness. Realize its profound principles. If this Way is not clarified, all will be in vain.

November, 1883

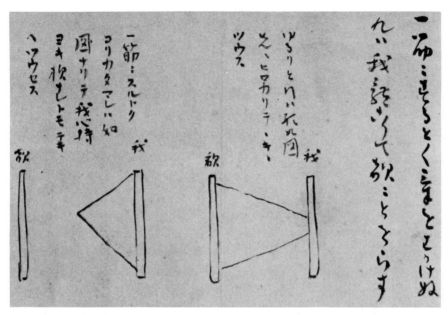

Section from Tesshu's original manuscript.

HOW TO PROJECT KI IN SWORDSMANSHIP

If one fails to act boldly with sharply focused ki, the body stiffens and the opponent's defenses cannot be penetrated.

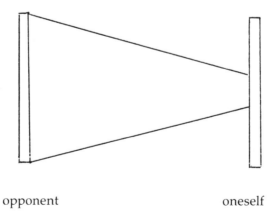

opponent   oneself

When one is stagnant, the opponent extends his ki, thus gaining an advantage.

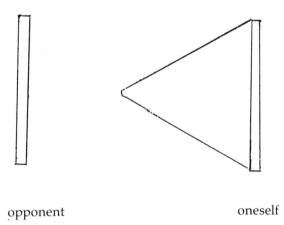

opponent   oneself

If one acts with unyielding determination, that confident state of mind projects one s ki toward the opponent.

Advancing
Without hesitation,
Ki power overcomes
all obstacles—
What a marvel!

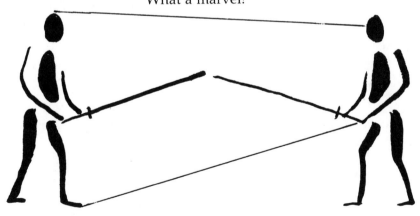

Lotus leaves rounder than the roundest mirror;
Water chestnut spines sharper than the sharpest drill.[12]

What does this Zen poem have in common with swordsmanship? The round leaves symbolize an immovable mind that reacts freely to any circumstance; the needle-like spines of a water chestnut stand for a sharp mind that responds at precisely the right moment. In order to strike the opponent, the attack must be razor sharp. A sharp mind emerges from a round mind; this is so because both roundness and sharpness are contained in a mind that abides nowhere. Practice diligently to attain these marvelous techniques; fully experience the depths of roundness and sharpness.

EXPLANATION OF THE MUTO RYU

Swordsmen train diligently to reach the ultimate state of "no-enemy." To focus on the relative strength or weakness of an opponent is to lose the state of no-enemy. All depends on mind. If one imagines the opponent to be skillful, the mind freezes and the sword is held back; if one imagines the opponent to be weak, the mind is open and the sword is unhindered. This is proof that nothing exists outside the mind. A swordsman may practice earnestly for many years, but if he is only moving the body and vacantly swinging the sword, his training is worthless. Based on my insights I have established what I call the "No-Sword School." Outside the mind there is no sword—this is "no-sword." "No-sword" means "no-mind"; "no mind" means a "mind that abides nowhere." If the mind stops, the opponent appears; if the mind remains fluid, no enemy exists. This is the essence of Mencius's saying, "Universal ki fills every inch of heaven and earth"—in other words "no-enemy." Practice day and night and you will attain the state of no-enemy. Train harder and harder!

April 10, 1884

THE SECRET ART OF THE CARPENTER'S PLANE

Use of a carpenter's plane involves three operations: rough, intermediate, and fine. In rough planing the body is braced, the abdomen tightened, the hips set, equal amounts of strength put into the hands, and the plane made. In short, strength is put into the entire body and one cannot relax. If one does not move forcefully a rough planing cannot be done.

Next, an intermediate planing is made. This time one must not use all his power. The natural touch of the hands controls increases and decreases in pressure. This level is preparation for the next step. However, if the continuity from rough planing to intermediate planing is broken through a lack of concentration the work cannot be properly executed.

From intermediate planing one moves to fine planing. Here, irregularities left from the previous steps are smoothed out. If it happens to be a pillar one is working on, one must go from top to bottom with one turn of the plane. While progressing from top to bottom, it is essential to keep the heart in perfect order. If the heart is not in order, various irregularities will appear and the work cannot be completed successfully. Proper control is the key.

Mind, body, and technique must function together in the same manner. "Mind, body, and technique" correspond to "plane, carpenter, and pillar." If one thinks the carpenter does the planing, of what use is the plane? If one thinks the plane does the planing, of what use is the pillar? Mind, body, and technique function together in a way similar to that of plane, carpenter, and pillar; if that interdependence is not understood, one will not be able to produce a good pillar regardless of how long one practices with a carpenter's plane. In order to create a good pillar, rough planing must be practiced first. Once that step is mastered, the next two steps can be mastered.

Fine planing is the "secret technique." That secret technique is nothing special. Mind, body, and technique are ultimately forgotten and one proceeds smoothly until the work is complete. To no longer think about finishing the plane and to no longer talk about technique or anything else is a marvelous state. It is futile to ask how to attain this—fine planing can only be learned by oneself; it can never be gotten from another.

April, 1884

ADMONITIONS FOR NEW ENTRANTS

To practice swordsmanship means to enter a training hall. It consists of much more than going in and out of a school room. It is a pledge made between teacher and student. The reason for this is that in swordsmanship instruction is imparted directly, face-to-face, from teacher to student. To receive that kind of individual instruction a formal pledge must be made upon entry. The relationship of teacher and student is like that of father to son. Certain people consider this to be an exaggeration, but it is the proper attitude to take. While it is better to obtain one's own set of equipment, it is permissible to temporarily borrow equipment from the training hall.

Although swordsmanship practice includes learning how to conduct oneself in contests, more important is swordsmanship as a Way of training the body and of setting aright the mind in a polite and civilized manner. If, during the course of sword training, one's deportment is lax, it will produce negative results. A proper attitude is essential. These admonitions have been in effect for twenty years and should be common knowledge among swordsmen, but I have written them down for new entrants.

June, 1885

NOTE ON *KUMITACHI*[13]

Within these varied techniques there is deep meaning.
Cast off subject and object, function as one;
Abandon self and others, form a single sword.
Use the piercing eyes of Heaven and Earth
To see through your opponent's body.

The way to practice *kumitachi* is "seize and release, release and seize." "Seize" means to seize the opponent's ki; "release" means to release one's own ki. This is the tradition of the Itto Ryu.

CONTESTS WITH A WOODEN SWORD AND NO ARMOR

In the past the practice of swordsmanship in all schools was understood as practice with a wooden sword and no protective armor. However, about one hundred years ago most schools began to use helmets, gloves, and chest protectors. The reason for this change is that protective gear enables trainees to act with less inhibition and allows them to apply the techniques with full force—this is the sole advantage.

Contests conducted with a wooden sword and no armor are quite different from modern matches. In such contests, there is much more reserve because of the fear of injury; even a skilled swordsman is in danger of being struck. If one lacks comprehension of sharply executed maneuvers according to the tenet of "strength in weakness, weakness in strength," he will find it difficult to engage in contests with a wooden sword.

Generally in the past when swordsmen of rival schools faced each other, either a steel sword with the blade covered or a wooden sword was used. Nonetheless, there were countless instances of swordsmen being struck down and killed. Self-taught swordsmen who were injured did not suffer the great shame that those with a teacher felt when they suffered defeat.

In my Way "no-form" is necessary. Once countless technical variations are mastered and freely applied, there is nowhere the sword cannot strike. Without a doubt, it is the Way of Heaven for the strong to help the weak. Why then do present day schools make use of helmets, gloves, and other protective equipment, seeking nothing more than to emerge victorious in a match? Naturally, in these matches those who are agile will win and those who are not will lose; technical experts are rarely threatened.

In the case of contests conducted with a wooden sword and no armor, that condition alone necessitates a proper frame of mind. If one is not careful, it is very dangerous. While it may be possible for a few of those who practice exclusively with protective equipment for many years to overcome the spiritual force of their opponents, hot-blooded swordsmen who rely on physical strength and attack as if they are still wearing protective gear will quickly be injured in a contest with wooden swords. Reflect upon this deeply and there will be no need to worry about injury. In contests conducted with a wooden sword and no armor, those trying to kill or maim their opponent are not practicing the true principles of swordsmanship.

November, 1884

SWORDSMANSHIP AND ORDINARY MIND

In the *Doctrine of the Mean* it says, "When happiness, anger, sorrow, and pleasure do not arise, it is termed 'equilibrium.' When those elements do appear and one acts accordingly, it is termed 'harmony.'" In other words, "equilibrium" is "ordinary mind." When there is happiness, be happy. When there is anger, be angry. When there is sorrow, be sad. When there is pleasure, rejoice in it. This is acting accordingly free of hindrance. Swordsmanship is exactly the same. When the opponent comes, follow him; transform his attack into your victory by acting accordingly. Here "ordinary mind" appears.

January 3, 1885

CERTIFICATE OF TRANSMISSION

You have perceived the root of the Way of the Sword. It is said, "Stand in the midst of the four corners and eight directions, horizontal and vertical, up and down, and pierce them all!" The patriarchs of our school realized that state and transmitted it. Heaven is yang. Yang continually descends as yin. Earth is yin. Yin develops and gives birth to yang. Thus spring returns at the appropriate time,

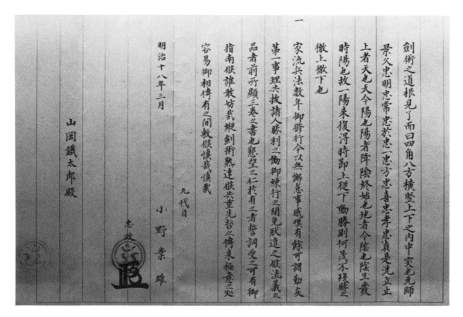

Certificate of transmission presented to Tesshu by Ono Nario.

following the dictates of heaven and the movements of the earth. This can never be obstructed; it permeates every hemisphere. For many years you have ceaselessly practiced the methods of our school. This is admirable indeed, a fine example of supreme effort. Out of many, you alone have extracted the first principle of particular and universal, grasped the real dimensions of victory, and are advanced sufficiently to receive a full teaching license. Three scrolls cataloging the techniques and codes of our school have already been presented to you. Your entreaties have been sincere, your pledges sound, and your petitions granted. Can anyone object to this presentation? Even though you have mastered swordsmanship, do not neglect the traditions of your enlightened predecessors. This document certifies the transmission of the ultimate teachings. Guard it carefully! Guard it carefully![14]

Ono Nario

March, 1885

EXPLANATION OF THE NAME MUTO RYU

"No-sword" means "outside the mind there is no sword"; in other words, "the three worlds are one Mind." One Mind means that both inside and outside there is not one thing. Therefore, when an opponent is confronted there is no enemy in front and no self behind. Miraculously, all boundaries are extinguished and no trace remains. This is the meaning of the name "No-Sword School."

From the three worlds of past, present, and future to the manifestation of all phenomena there is not one entity that is not Mind. That Mind is markless from start to finish; it functions as an inexhaustible treasure. Mind is exceedingly difficult to grasp: look for it in the east and it vanishes in the west; seek it in the south and it departs from the north. It possesses a divine freedom that even heaven cannot contain.

When that level is attained one discovers "a single sword against the cold sky." Face the enemy as if he were not there; roam freely through the universe like the golden-winged Garuda King. When that wonderful state is actualized it is a great marvel, permeating all things with life.

One's actions in everyday life should be conducted in a similar manner. Absolute freedom is not being hindered by anything. When sitting, sit; when walking, walk. Speech, silence, movement, stillness—all arise from the same source. The cutting edge of the Mind-sword is unequalled.

May 18, 1885

NOTE ON THE PRACTICE OF MUTO RYU SWORDSMANSHIP

In the past, such swordsmen as Tsukahara Bokuden,[15] Ito Ittosai, Miyamoto Musashi, and many others traveled throughout the land practicing in order to perfect their technique. Facing each other with live blades or thick wooden swords, they engaged in countless battles. Not a few of them lost their lives practicing in that way. Why did they do so? It may seem foolish to throw one's life away, but to those on that path it is the only method. If one is reluctant to risk his life in any endeavor, there is no way the truth will be found. Mere good fortune is not enough.

The approach of my Muto Ryu is similar; I do not want the teachings of our predecessors to be abandoned. For advanced swordsmen, contests with swordsmen of other schools is permitted, providing the match is conducted with a wooden sword and no armor. Any swordsman who agrees to this condition and applies for a contest will gladly be received without delay.

June, 1885

TESSHU'S SONGS OF THE WAY

Like many masters, Tesshu composed a number of *doka*, "songs of the Way," to express his teaching. Tesshu's Mt. Fuji doka (p. 45) is considered a modern classic of Zen poetry, a favorite verse of D. T. Suzuki and Nishida Kitaro, two of Japan's greatest thinkers. The first selections presented here cover swordsmanship, while the rest are concerned with more general themes.

> If your mind
> is not projected
> into your hands
> even 10,000 techniques
> will be useless.

Against an opponent's sword
assume no stance,
and keep your mind unmoved;
that is the place
of victory.

Swordsmanship:
I am not struck
nor is my opponent hit;
unobstructed I move in
and attain the ultimate.

Where swords meet
throw off illusion;
abandon yourself
and you will tread
on the living path.

The form which arises
from no-mind
stands in the center of things;
blows come but do not connect—
what a marvel!

Spirit, swift;
mind, calm;
body, light;
eyes, clear;
technique, decisive!

Self-centered thoughts
are reflecterd as
clearly as in a mirror;
let others see them,
and you will be making a fool of yourself.

Piled up high,
the snowman (just like everyone else)
after a few days.
goes somewhere
without a trace.

After death
you go to hell
but die again
and the Devil and his minions
will squawk (for mercy)!

Do not desire money,
do not depend on empty principles,
do not seek fame:
just go with what you have
and you will pass safely through this world.

The heart of things
which cannot be seen with the eyes—
that is where the seed of Buddha lies:
make it grow and grow
and truth will be yours.

"No more *sake* for you"
(my doctor declared)
but look at how tattered my sleeves are[16]—
pour me some, please;
full my cup again and again.

Inscription on a Painting of a Taoist Immortal
Ride the heavens far above
the world's folly
on the back of a crane:
sport for a thousand years,
enjoying every minute!

Inscription on a Painting of a Woodcutter
Chop and chop away
at grief and sorrow
with each hard whack;
hidden away among the flowers and crimson leaves,
forgetting about the world's petty troubles.

A Lot
The sound of coaches
carrying people on the move
never ceases;
no matter how much you go, though,
someday you must return.

A Little
Over a few years
let intimacy
ripen naturally—
the number of friends will be small
but the quality will be very large.

Lazy Fellow
"This country is supposed
to have 84,000 gods,
but the only one
who visits here
is the god of poverty!"

The God of Poverty Replies
"Gambling away all your money,
Guzzling *sake*,
leading an idle life—
there is no better place
for me to stay!"

Tobacco Shop
The tobacco leaves
so nicely cut,
such a fine color
and fragrance;
one good puff, though,
and all that is left is ash.

CATALOGS OF TECHNIQUES (MOKUROKU)

Tesshu awarded certification to a few of his senior disciples in the form of two *mokuroku*, catalogs of techniques. Evidently, the actual contents of the catalogs were transmitted orally and the certificates that Tesshu wrote consisted only of the titles of the mokuroku. The two catalogs were likely based on Itto Ryu catalogs handed down by the various subschools. The catalog translated here is based on the original in Tesshu's own hand. Such catalogs are composed in extremely cryptic style and are meant to be puzzled out by the swordsman as he practices.

It is unclear exactly how many swordsmen received such certificates. Thirty-one are mentioned in extant Muto Ryu records, but at least one other person who received a certificate is not listed.

ITTO SHODEN MUTO RYU KANAJI MOKUROKU

One-Sword

From the one of "one-sword," ten elements arise; the ten elements are contained in the one. However myriad elements are counted, this tenet holds. Learn properly and see clearly; this is origin of "one-sword."

Although a hunter may not consciously "look" at the mountains as he pursues a deer, he still "sees" them. The hunter passes through mountain after mountain, but because his mind is set on the deer he does not notice them. And if the deer comes to a river it naturally leaps over it—what would happen if it hesitated to enter unknown territory? While it cannot be said that the mountains are not seen, it also cannot be said that they are seen. Kagehisa, the founder of our school, said about this, "After all, each mountain has been viewed" [i.e., seen once and remembered]. Armed with that knowledge, one is able to block off a mountain pass or close the mouth of a river depending on the situation. One also avoids chasing in the wrong direction.

Wind rustles the bush clover; soft, hard, strong, and weak places exist. React to the opponent's strength with weakness; seize decisively on the opponent's weakness to gain victory. The matching of strength with strength, weakness with weakness, stone with stone, and cloth with cloth [is not good]. When two stones are struck together, they fly apart and nothing is won; when cloth is rubbed with cloth, the great matter of life and death cannot be witnessed. In the Itto Ryu there is this tenet: "timing of no-timing."

Suigetsu, "Moon-water"

Even when water is scooped up in a ladle the moon is reflected in it. The moon's reflection is not lost as the water is passed from ladle to ladle. If one is disturbed, there can be no recognition; no moon appears in agitated water. If the mind is calm and the ladle steady, the moon's reflection is retained.

> Do not concentrate
> On striking your opponent.
> Deport yourself naturally
> Like moonbeams flooding
> Into a leaky cottage.

This state of mind is totally different from being caught with a stiff sword, terrified of defeat. One may be dissatisfied with a leaky cottage, but the same moon that illuminates the heavens naturally fills

Suigetsu, "Moon-Water." A well-known poem states:

> The moon does not think to be reflected,
> Nor does the water think to reflect,
> In the Hirosawa Pond.

When the moon reveals itself, it is immediately reflected on the water, yet the moon does not consciously seek out water and water makes no effort to hold the light. This reaction is spontaneous, in perfectly natural accord. The moon makes no distinctions, casting beams equally on oceans and drops of dew, pure springs and mud puddles. Such an unobstructed state of instant, untainted response is the ideal of both Zen and swordsmanship. Takuan, spiritual advisor to the Zen swordsman Yagyu Munenori, added this inscription to his calligraph of suigetsu:

> Buddhism is like the moon in the water.

it with light. Similarly, by not trying to protect oneself and ignoring imagined weakpoints, one can attack the opponent and achieve victory. Unconcerned with guarding one's small self, charge toward the opponent. If one is troubled or confused in any degree, defeat is certain.

Honsho

There are three types of *honsho*: *shin*, *so*, and *gyo*. *Shin no honsho* is "original victory." *So no honsho* is "original rightness." *Gyo no honsho* is "original birth." Transmission has so and gyo aspects. An example of original rightness is the ability to hold down and control at will the point of attack. A sword that arises and develops from yang is inherently incapable of sweeping things away; original birth brings things to life and fosters true growth. To act in accordance with spiritual knowledge enables one to be free of strain and discord. Right from the beginning, victory is ours; even if a blunder is made, there will be no danger. One who passes along shin no honsho, "the original victory," to his disciples leaves an inheritance more precious than gold.

Zanshin

Zanshin, "unbroken concentration," means following up. Victory consists of moving with confidence directly to the place of victory. A single, unstoppable strike must be executed without delay; no mind lingers, all thoughts are cast off, and one advances directly devoid of confusion. During practice, zanshin is frequently misused by conceited swordsmen who employ it as a bluff. Those who are aware of that kind of posturing attain victory through the principle of "attack while waiting, wait during attack." Do not use imitation zanshin. A skillful opponent can anticipate such false zanshin, adjust his timing, and win the match. Guard against this situation at all times. Zanshin is not "unbroken concentration on victory."

Uchi-ore Soto-ore

The best place to cut is along the inner seam (*uchi-ore*). Even when a large cut is made along the outer seam (*soto-ore*), at least fifty percent of the inner seam should remain. Although any section [of the body] may be struck, avoid small-scale movements.

The Eight Angles

An illustration of "eight angles": When a single stance, for example, gedan is assumed, do not fix exclusively on that angle. Look to the left and find the yin sword; protect the front and attain original awakening. If one is backed by allies this type of insight cannot occur. Single-minded, unconfused, straightforward movement is expressed as "one-sword." Know the place of victory and set oneself squarely in the midst of life and death. Fail to attain this by oneself and nothing can be accomplished. That is a great pity.

The Master's Teaching

One who claims to have thoroughly learned his master's techniques while disregarding his master's teaching, relying instead on his own talents, is worse than a fool. Such a person is a mere shadow of his teacher. How can he be described? He is like a bridge on a koto, nothing more than a piece of equipment. Teachers must exercise especial caution not to impart their wisdom to those who are not ready for it.

Where to Aim the Eyes (*Kento*)

"Look" (*ken*) is that which can be seen. If the strike can be clearly seen emerging from yin, its intended direction can be known. "Hit" (*to*) means imagining one's own blow arising from yin and finding its mark in a flash. Hence, do not cling to gestures; attack while waiting, that is, instantly adjust to conditions. The ultimate principles of swordsmanship are written down in many volumes, but words alone will never ensure victory. One may never read a word in any manual, but if he conducts himself properly, is there anything he lacks? Adapt to changing circumstances like water. Do not rely on one technique; cast off preconceptions and practice afresh, each day, every day.

Do not think that
This is all there is.
More and more
Wonderful teachings exist—
The sword is unfathomable.

The world is wide,
Full of happenings.
Keep that in mind
And never believe
"I'm the only one who knows."

BUSHIDO

My Bushido is based on the principles of Buddhism. That teaching covers all aspects of human life. There are different systems in the world that profess many kinds of virtues; all are good but only those people who actually put those virtues into practice are observing Bushido.

Bushido is the proper way of life for the Japanese. In order to learn the Way, forget about self and awaken to the truth. Drop off illusion, clarify heaven and earth, look at things the way they really are and realize no-self.

Exerting self is a mistake. Everyone originated from the same source and inherited a body from his or her parents who, in turn, received life from their mothers and fathers. We should not say "myself"—in truth, there is no such thing. The expectant mother carries her child for ten months (forty weeks), nourishing it with her own breath and blood. It is a union of love. When there is no thought of self, true Bushido develops. Harmony is the basis of heaven and earth and the Great Way for human beings. All things, everywhere, are interdependent. Nothing exists of itself. Due to the efforts of all sentient beings we are able to live. Therefore, we must have compassion for all living things. The myriad beings of the six worlds—gods, humans, beasts, ghosts, demons, and devils—are our relatives and friends.

The main element of Bushido is gratitude—gratitude toward parents and ancestors, gratitude toward sentient beings, gratitude toward the leader of the nation, and gratitude toward the Three Treasures.

Initially, we are grateful for the things that are near to us—our parents, sentient beings, the leader of the nation. Then we should be grateful for the things that cannot be seen—the Three Treasures: Buddha, Dharma, and Sangha. Bushido is derived from the second Treasure. Dharma is the Law of the universe and the mother of all Buddhas. It is incomprehensibly vast; since it is without form or shape it cannot be understood easily. Heaven and earth cannot contain it, a torrent of words cannot describe it. To grasp the Dharma, look into things near at hand and examine your heart. There is no need to search elsewhere. People pay homage to different gods and buddhas, but in reality all gods and buddhas are one.

The four gratitudes must be put into practice in society; this is the essence of my Bushido. However, in modern society many care for nothing but their own welfare and engage in any type of business or even thievery to get ahead. Public servants are little better. They are stealing their salaries, wanting to be served rather than to serve. What do these people know about Bushido?

Desire for fame and wealth has replaced the desire for enlightenment. Modern science has captivated selfish people who prefer its abstractions to human emotion. Throughout our history our country has imported many ideas. Some were good and became part of

Tesshu was fond of portraying an old couple sitting peacefully together accompanied by the inscription:

> You'll reach one hundred,
> I'll reach ninety-nine,
> As our hair turns white
> together.

"Others first" is the basis of harmonious social relationships, and a good companion is real treasure. Tesshu developed the greatest respect for his wife and often said to his friends that he could have accomplished nothing without her help.

our culture; yet it seems that the so-called modern sciences are slowly poisoning the nation.

Today everyone is arguing about "rights"—government rights, individual rights, property rights, and so on. It is impossible to spell out everything within the science of law; so many points are unclear that the distinction between proper and improper is blurred. Legalism will destroy initiative and eliminate compassion; trust, loyalty, honor, love, humility, and other virtues can never be legislated. Bushido alone nurtures those virtues. Law can never be more than an artifice; Bushido is the true Law of the spirit.

We must look after each other without regard to our own welfare, kill selfish desires, bravely face all enemies, and keep a stainless mind—this is Bushido.[17]

ON CALLIGRAPHY

Many years ago, around 1865, I was worshiping at the national temple in Otowa when I happened to notice some exquisite calligraphy displayed in one corner. The characters were free of worldliness and the brushwork pure and fresh; it was truly the work of an "ascending dragon." Upon examination, I discovered that the piece was from the hand of the Buddhist Patriarch, Kobo Daishi. I cannot express the sublime beauty present in his writing and I have never been able to forget it.

Two *ichigyo mono*, one line sayings.
Left, Music and poetry: creations of the gods.
Right, A humble hut jammed with books and calligraphy.

Thereafter, I studied various styles of calligraphy both by priests and laymen, copying them whenever I had the opportunity. This continued for a number of years until I attained a certain degree of mastery. That was in 1872 or 3.

On March 30, 1880, I realized the true meaning of swordsmanship and Zen. Since deep attainment enables one to comprehend many things, I simultaneously grasped the essence of calligraphy. Although I now know the secret I cannot explain it in words. Who in this world can?

Some have criticized my calligraphy saying, "Yamaoka Tesshu's calligraphy does not fit into any accepted school. It is not clear whether it is calligraphy or painting." It is true that I do not belong to any particular school. Regardless of one's affiliation, as long as the calligraphy reflects the true state of one's mind that is sufficient. At present my calligraphy belongs to the "Tesshu School."

THE ESSENCE OF BUDDHISM

When the essence of Buddhism is penetrated with clear insight, all things—heaven, earth, mountains, rivers, riches, poverty, men, women—are seen exactly as they are. Officers serve, merchants sell, farmers plow, fishermen fish; each accomplishes his or her work without hindrance. Such realization occurs in a flash—"Walking along the Great Way beneath a clear blue sky."

With that kind of Mind, one is master of the three worlds even though he or she lives in a hut or dwells in poverty. Both samsara and nirvana are transcended; officer, merchant, farmer, fisherman— the labor of each is without equal in heaven and earth. All operate in unfettered samadhi: "This very body is Buddha"; "This world of sorrow is actually paradise."

Three *gaku*, horizontally mounted calligraphy. *Top*,
The First Barrier. *Bottom*, Silence is Eloquent. *Next page*,
Iron Ox Function. This is in *tensho*, ancient seal-type
characters. "Iron Ox Function" is the subject of case
thirty-eight of the *Hekiganroku*. It symbolizes unsurpassed
power and irrepressible determination.

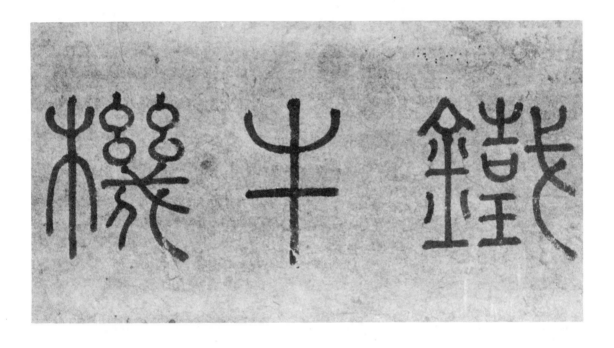

Birthright

Buddhism fosters Mind-essence and actualizes it in the world. It is the birthright every individual possesses from the beginning, belonging to no one else. Each person contains a boundless treasure within him- or herself. Yet of all the billions of people on earth, how many are aware of their innate wealth? It is a great pity that people mistakenly value gold, silver, and diamonds rather than their own true riches. One who regains his birthright will be master of three thousand worlds.

In the present age, worldly knowledge increases month by month while marvelous knowledge of "non-action" decreases daily. What is "non-action?" Fighting furiously in the midst of a raging battle without a hair out of place. An ancient said, "All day not a single thing is done; all day not a word is spoken." The *Lotus Sutra* states: "Awake or asleep, no difference." Working in the world, pressed by business, bustling here and there, is the same as snoring loudly while peacefully drunk—both are places of the "solitary splendor of non-action."

Where are you now? Climb the treasure mountain and do not return empty-handed.

NOTES

1. "Particular" (*ji*) is a "manifestation," i.e., an event or object in time and space; "universal" (*ri*) is the underlying "principle"—ji and ri can also be characterized as form and formlessness, relative and absolute, experience and truth. In all of the Ways, the ideal is to link the particular technique to the universal truth.

2. In Tesshu's writings "natural" (*shizen* or *jinen*) means "of itself without conscious effort" and "unfolding spontaneously according to ri."

3. This of course was backdated to coincide with the date of Tesshu's enlightenment. It was actually composed on March 30, 1883. There is another version on page 130.

4. This document marks the formal creation of the Muto Ryu. As mentioned in Chapter 2, Tesshu considered himself to be a restorer rather than an innovator, and the selection of the name mu-to, no-sword, was not novel. Yagyu Tajima no kami Munenori, sixteenth master of the Yagyu Shinkage Ryu, reportedly said, "If my school did not already have a name, I would call it the Muto Ryu."

5. *Myo* is a wonder beyond analytical understanding; it connotes spontaneity and creativity.

6. Huge mythical dragon-eating birds that dwell on Mt. Sumeru, center of the Buddhist universe.

7. This refers to the final meeting of Kusunoki Masashige and the Zen master, Gokushun. The day before he was to face the overwhelming forces of his enemy Ashikaga, Kusunoki visited Gokushun and asked, "How should I stand between life and death?" Gokushun replied, "Cut off dualism and keep a single sword against the cold sky."

8. See illustrations on pages 20 and 156.

9. One of Tesshu's most treasured possessions, this wooden sword is believed to have been carved by Ittosai. On it were five inscriptions written in red ink:

"Timing of no-timing" was written on the end; underneath, on the edge, was written "control" and "victory"; near the hilt, "attack" was written in front of the sword guard and "control" was written behind it. Kogeta Yasumada, an influential government official, was Tesshu's long-time disciple-friend-supporter. Following Koteta's death, the shuin tachi was passed to Yanagita Ganjiro.

10. This is a verse from the forty-fourth case of the koan collection *Hekinganroku*. "Look at the marvelous truth manifest right here now."

11. Ito Ittosai Kagehisa, founder of the Itto Ryu, flourished in the beginning of the Tokugawa period, but very little else is known for certain about his life. For Tesshu, Ittosai symbolized the classical teachings of the past, and he carefully recorded both the written and oral traditions of the Itto Ryu.

12. A saying of the Daie Soko (1089–1163).

13. "Paired techniques," i.e., fixed forms practiced in unison with a partner. Tesshu's Muto Ryu kata were derived from classical Itto Ryu forms.

14. On January 30, 1881, Asari Gimei presented Tesshu with a formal certificate designating him as thirteenth Headmaster of the Nakanishi-ha Itto Ryu. In 1885, Ono Nario (Tadamasa), then living in retirement and without an heir, decided to name Tesshu—originally of the Ono clan and Nario's distant relative—tenth Headmaster of the Ono Itto Ryu.

Nario also presented Tesshu with the heirloom *"Kamewari Ken."* This extraordinary "pot-cleaving sword," said to have been forged by the master smith Ichijimonji, derived its name from the following incidents: When Ittosai was a young man, he was a disciple of the Shinto priest-swordsman Oribe. One day, Oribe called Ittosai over and took down the sword set before the altar. Oribe then dropped the blade over one of the large pots used to brew and store sacred sake. The blade cut straight to the bottom of the pot. Oribe made a present of this wonderful sword to his promising pupil. A few nights later, bandits attempted to ransack the shrine. Grabbing his still handle-less sword by its base, Ittosai quickly dispatched seven of the rude intruders. One bandit tried to hide in one of the big pots. With one tremendous cut, Ittosai cleft both the pot and the bandit cleanly in two.

The sword was given to Ittosai's top disciple and heir Ono Tadaaki, and it was passed to each successive headmaster until it came down to Tesshu. Unfortunately, Tesshu had no formal heir and, according to a document by Deishu, Tesshu's wife donated it to the famous Toshogu shrine in Nikko. However, it is no longer there and its whereabouts are unknown (one account states that it perished in one of the Zensho-an fires).

15. The *mutekatsu* of Tsukahara Bokuden is well-known. Once Bokuden happened to be on a small ferry boat when another swordsman began boasting of his prowess. While the braggart carried on, Bokuden dozed off. This angered the other swordsman who shook Bokuden, demanding to know what style he followed.

Bokuden told him, "The 'Victory-without-using-one's-hands' (mutekatsu) School." The rowdy swordsman challenged Bokuden to display such swordsmanship. Bokuden agreed, but suggested they stop at an island to avoid injury to the other passengers. The ferry made a detour to a nearby island. As soon as the boat reached the shore, the man leaped off, drew his sword, and assumed his stance. Bokuden stood up and appeared ready to follow his opponent when he suddenly grabbed an oar and precipitately pushed the boat back into the river. He yelled to the stranded swordsman, "This is defeating the enemy without using your hands."

16. ". . . but look at how tattered my sleeves are": meaning, "My body is all worn out and ready to go anyway, so what is the worry?"

17. This and the following three pieces are excerpts from talks and essays edited by Tesshu's disciples.